THE
BASS
STYLE
RESOURCE

MW00560796

a comprehensive guide
to exploring new techniques and
styles from heavy metal to jazz

DAVE OVERTHROW

CD recorded by Collin Tilton at Bar None Studio, Northford, CT
Dave Overthrow (bass), Kurt Berglund (drums), Morgan Kelsey (keyboard), Burgess Speed (guitar)

Cover photographs courtesy of (clockwise from top): Fender Musical Instruments, Andrew Kepert, Music Man, Fender Musical Instruments, and Schecter Guitar Research

Alfred

Alfred Music Publishing Co., Inc.
P.O. Box 10003
Van Nuys, CA 91410-0003
alfred.com

ISBN-10: 0-7390-8909-9 (Book & CD)
ISBN-13: 978-0-7390-8909-5 (Book & CD)

CONTENTS

++

ABOUT THE AUTHOR

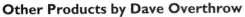

Dave Overthrow has been a performer for over 30 years. He attended Berklee College of Music and earned a jazz performance degree from Western Connecticut State University. Dave is the author of many instructional books and DVDs, all published by Alfred Music Publishing. The Dave Overthrow Band has released two CDs, *In the Pocket* and *2 Hot to Touch*. In addition to serving a three-year stint as a staff writer for *Bass Guitar Magazine*, Dave is the Director of Music and head of Jazz Studies at the Canterbury School in New Milford, CT. Dave's work has led him to performances with Stanley Clarke, Mike Stern, Zakk Wylde, Trey Anastasio, and others. Dave Overthrow plays Ron Blake handmade basses, DR Handmade Strings, and SWR bass amplifiers. Check out Dave's website at daveoverthrow.com.

PHOTO COURTESY OF WORKSHOPLIVE.COM

Other Products by Dave Overthrow
(all titles published by Alfred Music Publishing):

Books

Beginning Electric Bass (#19362)

Intermediate Electric Bass (#19359)

Mastering Electric Bass (#19356)

30-Day Bass Workout (#20398)

Slap & Pop Bass (#21904)

Beginning Blues Bass (#24415)

Beginning Bass For Adults (#27310)

The Total Jazz Bassist (#26063)

The Total Funk Bassist (#32659)

Instructional DVDs

Beginning Electric Bass (#22889)

Beginning Blues Bass (#24416)

30-Day Bass Workout (#24211)

Acknowledgements
Thanks to Kurt Berglund (drums), Morgan Kelsey (keyboard), and Burgess Speed (guitar) for playing on the CD that accompanies this book.

Track 1

A compact disc is included with this book. This disc can make learning with the book easier and more enjoyable. The symbol shown at the left appears next to every example that is on the CD. Use the CD to help ensure that you're capturing the feel of the examples, interpreting the rhythms correctly, and so on. The track number below the symbol corresponds directly to the example you want to hear. Track 1 is a tuning track that will help you tune your bass to the CD.

INTRODUCTION

+ +

Welcome to *The Bass Style Resource*, a survey of many different musical styles and techniques that will help you become a more versatile musician. Why is versatility important for a bassist? All other factors being equal, versatility helps you stand out from other players. Imagine you're auditioning bass players for your band. The first player is a slap & pop specialist with incredible chops. His playing is impressive at first, but he plays the same thing on every song. The second player doesn't blow you away at first, but he listens to each of your songs and tries to play what sounds best. On one song, he plays a little bit funky, on another, he plays a deep reggae groove with lots of space, and on the next, he gets jazzy. Which player would you hire?

Music is such a vast topic that it's natural to specialize in your studies. Perhaps you think you'll learn faster and get a gig sooner if you just focus on blues bass. You'd probably start with topics like the blues scale, dominant 7th chords, and the 12-bar blues form. There is nothing wrong with this approach—all of these topics are worth learning—but *The Bass Style Resource* uses a different tactic, based on real-world experience. Instead of just learning about the blues, you'll study other styles like rock, reggae, funk, and jazz. Soon, you'll realize these other styles have much in common with the blues, and by branching out in your studies, you will actually have a deeper understanding of the blues and music in general.

If you are knowledgeable about many genres, able to adapt to different styles, able to execute a variety of techniques, and are open-minded about new music, then you will appeal to a larger group of potential musical collaborators. Well-rounded musicians are always in demand. Versatility is especially important to session players, as they play behind artists of many different styles. Touring bassists are able to go out on the road with many different bands if they are versatile in terms of style. Even amateur bass players who play club gigs on weekends have more opportunities if they are versatile and open-minded.

This book is designed to help any bassist of any level to become a versatile player. It is helpful to already be familiar with standard music notation. The first few chapters discuss important music theory that you should be able to translate onto the bass. The main section of this book is dedicated to playing grooves in different styles such as rock, blues, old school funk, modern funk, reggae, ska, jazz, and more. You'll also learn the techniques used by bass players in these styles such as fingerstyle funk, slap & pop, double thumping, double plucking, playing chords on the bass, tapping, and soloing.

I hope you enjoy the book and that the bass grooves in this book inspire you to create some of your own in each style.

CHAPTER ONE
GETTING STARTED

+ +

Half Steps and Whole Steps

A *half step* is the distance of one fret on the bass and is the smallest *interval* (distance between two notes) in music. A *whole step* is an interval of two half steps, or two frets on the bass. Half steps and whole steps are the building blocks for all the chords and scales you'll find throughout this book. Check out the fretboard diagram below.

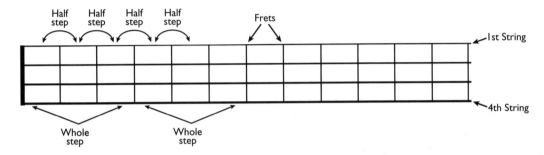

The Notes of the Fretboard

The next step is to learn the *musical alphabet*: A–B–C–D–E–F–G. Once you pass G, the cycle repeats, beginning on A again. Moving through the alphabet (A–B–C, etc.), the *pitches* ascend and sound higher (pitch refers to the highness or lowness of musical sound). Moving in reverse alphabetical order (C–B–A), the pitches descend and sound lower. The fretboard diagram below shows where the notes are located on the fretboard. Notice the names of the open strings shown in the diagram.

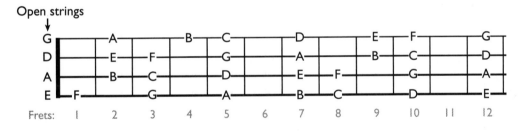

Time Signatures

A *time signature* indicates how many beats are in each measure and consists of two numbers, one on top of the other. The top number tells you how many beats are in each measure, and the bottom number tells you what kind of note gets one beat.

$\frac{4}{4}$ = 4 beats per measure
Quarter note ♩ = one beat

$\frac{3}{4}$ = 3 beats per measure
Quarter note ♩ = one beat

$\frac{6}{8}$ = 6 beats per measure
Eighth note ♪ = one beat

Since $\frac{4}{4}$ is the most commonly used time signature, it is referred to as *common time* and is sometimes indicated with a 𝄴.

Triplets and Swing Eighths

Triplets consist of three notes in the time of two. For example, three *eighth-note triplets* add up to one beat, compared with two regular, or *straight*, eighth notes per beat. *Swing eighths* consist of eighth-note triplets with the first two tied together. Typically, *Swing 8ths* appears at the beginning of a song to indicate all eighth notes should be interpreted as swing eighths. The following example shows the different types of eighth notes.

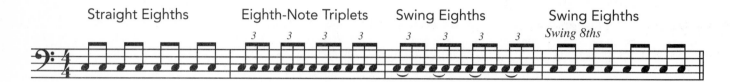

Reading Bass Tablature

Tablature, or TAB, indicates where notes are located on the fretboard. The four lines of the TAB staff represent the four strings of the bass. The top line represents the 1st string (G), the second line represents the 2nd string (D), the third line represents the 3rd string (A), and the bottom line represents the 4th string (E). The numbers on the lines tell you which fret to play. The numbers underneath the TAB tell you which left-hand finger to use. (The left-hand fingers are numbered 1 through 4, starting with the index finger.) The examples in this book are all presented in both standard music notation and TAB.

Compare the standard music notation and TAB shown to the right. The first note is F. The TAB indicates the note should be played on the 3rd fret of the 2nd string. The second note is C, 5th fret of the 1st string, and the third note is C, 3rd fret of the 3rd string.

Some players only read TAB and never learn standard music notation. While TAB is easy to learn, it does have drawbacks: it does not tell you what rhythm to play, and it only allows you to read music written specifically for bass. To be the most versatile player, you should learn both standard music notation and TAB.

Reading Chord Symbols

A *chord* consists of three or more notes played simultaneously. Chords are indicated by using *chord symbols* located above the staff. The chord symbol indicates which chord is being played at that moment. A series of chords is called a *chord progression* or *changes*. Bass players typically play only one note at a time, outlining the different chord tones. Playing the notes of a chord one at a time instead of together is called *arpeggiation*.

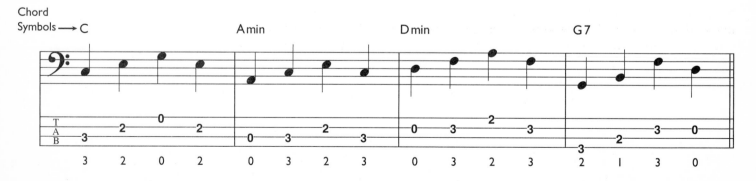

CHAPTER TWO
THE GROOVE

+ +

The Power of the Groove

When the bass player is "locked in" with the drummer and the crowd is gettin' down, that's the power of the groove. Whatever the genre—rock, soul, funk, country—great bass lines make people want to tap their feet, clap their hands, or get up and dance. Do not judge bass players by how many notes they play or how fast their hands move. It all comes down to *feeling:* Does the bass line make you want to move your body?

Always strive to keep the groove regardless of how many notes you're playing or which techniques you are incorporating into your bass line. Great players like James Jamerson, Larry Graham, and Jaco Pastorius are able to play complex and innovative bass lines without ever sacrificing the groove. These musicians lay down grooves that can be *felt* by the body, not just heard with the ears.

The Interpretation of Time

It's impossible to groove if you don't have a good sense of time. If you listen to a lot of bass players, however, you'll hear that each has a different sense of time. Some bassists play slightly behind the beat, some play slightly ahead of the beat, and others play right on the beat. This does not mean that some are right and some are wrong, but rather that each has his or her own interpretation of time. Everyone has a different personality and approach to playing music. Some are more relaxed, some are more aggressive, and some are exactly to the point. A versatile bassist listens to the other musicians, especially the drummer, and interprets time in a way that sounds best in that situation.

Playing with a Metronome

A *metronome* is a device that generates a steady clicking sound at the tempo of your choice. Practicing with a metronome will help you develop your sense of time and learn how to lock in with a drummer. If you are skeptical about practicing with a metronome, try this exercise: Imagine you're on stage, and the metronome is your drummer. Try to lock in with the "drummer" and create a solid groove. You'll find it is a fun and realistic way to practice. Even better, practice with a drum machine or jam track for more complex beats.

The Power of Silence

Music is a language. Like all languages, sometimes it is best to say nothing. Silence is an important part of the musical vocabulary. If you constantly play fast musical passages with no space, your playing will sound monotonous. Silence also allows the other members of the band to "get a word in edgewise." Good bass players know when to play and when to leave space. Listen to some of your favorite reggae bass lines and notice how much space you discover in the bass part. Silence can be very effective.

Playing with the Drummer

Here's a listening exercise for you. Listen to Tracks 2 and 3 on the accompanying CD;
compare the two bass parts below to the drum parts. Notice the drum part accents
certain beats (>), which we'll call *kicks*. Bass part [A] uses a constant eighth-note rhythm.
It is a technically correct bass part, but it does not feel "locked in" with the drummer.
Bass part [B] mixes up the rhythm to emphasize the same beats as the bass drum kicks,
resulting in a "locked in" feeling.

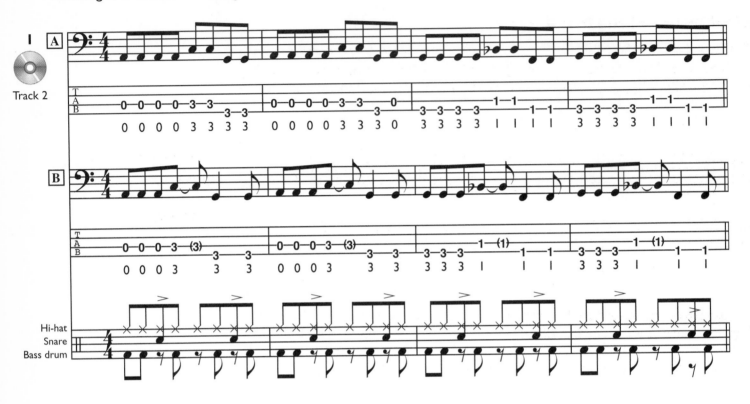

Here is another pair of bass lines with a drum part. Listen to how part [B] locks in with
the bass drum and snare drum kicks. Which bass line has a better groove?

8   The Bass Style Resource

CHAPTER THREE
THE MAJOR SCALE

+ +

Significance of the Major Scale

The *major scale* is the first scale you should learn, because every scale, chord, and mode you will learn can be defined relative to the major scale. The major scale consists of the following series of whole steps and half steps: Whole–Whole–Half–Whole–Whole–Whole–Half. Shown below is the C Major scale.

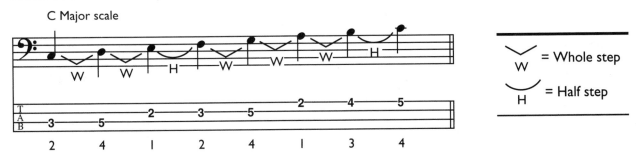

The pattern of whole steps and half steps is true for every major scale, all 12 of them. The fingering shown above is one that allows you to play the scale in one position.

To learn more about scales, check out *The Total Jazz Bassist* (#26063).

Intervals

An interval is the distance between two pitches. There are two parts to the name of an interval, one being an adjective and the second being a number. The adjectives used to name intervals are *major*, *minor*, *perfect*, *augmented*, and *diminished*. Numbers from 1 to 8 are used to describe intervals within an *octave* (the interval between a note and the next note of the same name). Intervals larger than an octave are known as *compound intervals* and use larger numbers such as 9, 10, 11, or 13. For now, we will stick to discussing the intervals within an octave. All intervals in a major scale are major intervals with the exception of the 4th and 5th, which are called perfect intervals. When a major interval is lowered by a half step, it becomes minor. When a minor interval is lowered by a half step, it becomes diminished. When a perfect interval is raised by a half step, it becomes augmented, and if lowered, it becomes diminished. Following are the intervals above the note C within an octave range.

Key Signatures

A *key signature* is a group of sharps or flats placed to the right of the clef on the staff. The number of sharps or flats tells you at a glance in what *key* a piece of music is written. A key is the tonal center of a song or scale. We'll begin by looking at the 12 *major* keys. (See page 18 for the *minor* keys and how they are *relative* to the major keys).

A bass line created with the notes of a C Major scale is in the key of C. The scale is built from the note C, so C is the *tonic* or *root*. If we build a major scale starting on the note G, the sequence of whole steps and half steps would result in one sharp, F♯. Therefore, the key signature for the key of G contains one sharp, F♯.

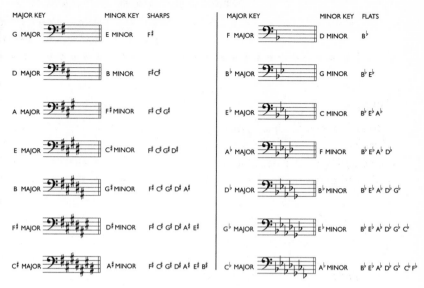

The Circle of 5ths

The *circle of 5ths* is a systematic way for you to become familiar with all 12 keys or major scales. The keys are in a clockwise arrangement of ascending perfect 5ths beginning with the key of C.

The key of C Major has no sharps or flats. As you move clockwise around the circle, each key is a perfect 5th above the previous and has one more sharp. If you start at C and move counterclockwise, each key is a perfect 5th below the previous and has one more flat. Notice that certain keys can be spelled using either sharps or flats; for example, G and F. These are known as *enharmonic keys*. They have exactly the same pitches and sound, but are written differently.

Many musicians often think of the circle of 5ths as the *circle of 4ths*, which is really a counterclockwise view of the circle. Moving down a 5th is the equivalent of moving up a 4th. Jazz players often prefer to view the circle this way, as many tunes use chord progressions that move through the flat keys in ascending 4ths (or descending 5ths).

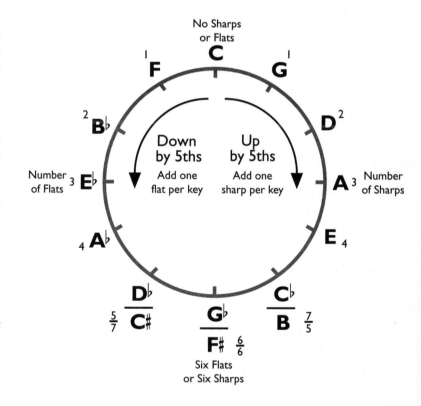

The circle of 5ths is shown above. Try to use this circle and practice chords and scales that you learn in all 12 keys.

CHAPTER FOUR
CHORDS

+ +

Triads

A *triad* is a chord that consists of three notes. Like the intervals, there are four types of triads: *major*, *minor*, *diminished*, and *augmented*. Let's look at a couple of methods for constructing each type. One possible fingering for each triad is shown in the TAB, and the fretboard diagrams to the right of each example show two more options.

Major Triad

A *major triad* is constructed by taking the 1st (the root), 3rd, and 5th scale degrees (1–3–5) of a major scale. A major triad can also be created by stacking two 3rds above the root, the first being a major 3rd (four half steps), and the second being a minor 3rd (three half steps).

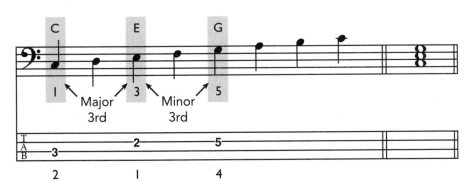
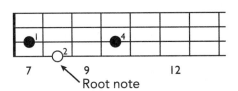
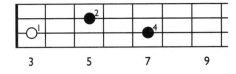

Minor Triad

A *minor triad* is constructed by taking the 1st, 3rd, and 5th scale degrees of a major scale and lowering the 3rd by a half step (♭3). A minor triad can also be created by stacking two 3rds above the root, the bottom 3rd being minor and the top 3rd being major.

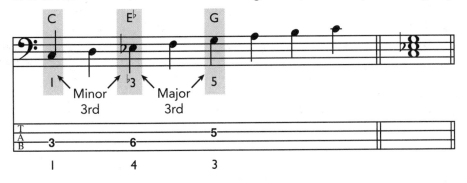
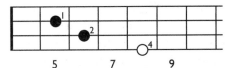
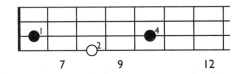

Diminished Triad

A *diminished triad* is constructed by taking the 1st, 3rd, and 5th scale degrees of a major scale and lowering both the 3rd and 5th by a half step (♭3, ♭5). A diminished triad can also be created by stacking two 3rds above the root, both the bottom 3rd and the top 3rd being minor.

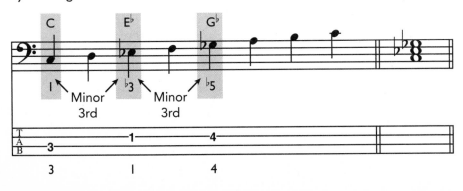
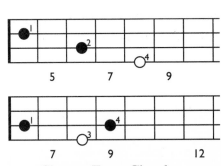

Augmented Triad

An *augmented triad* is constructed by taking the 1st, 3rd, and 5th scale degrees of a major scale and raising the 5th by a half step (♯5). An augmented triad can also be created by stacking two 3rds above the root, both the bottom 3rd and the top 3rd being major.

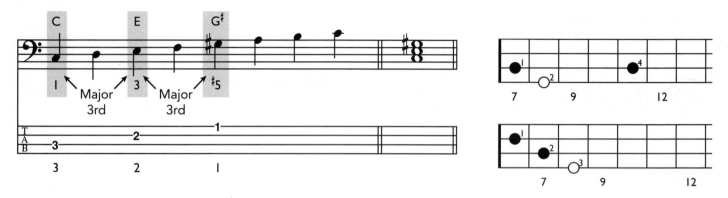

7th Chords

A *7th chord* consists of four notes. Let's look at five commonly used 7th chord types.

Major 7th

A *major 7th chord* is constructed by taking a major triad, or 1st, 3rd, and 5th of a major scale, and adding a major 7th interval above the root. The resulting scale degrees are 1, 3, 5, and 7. The intervals between chord tones are major 3rd–minor 3rd–major 3rd.

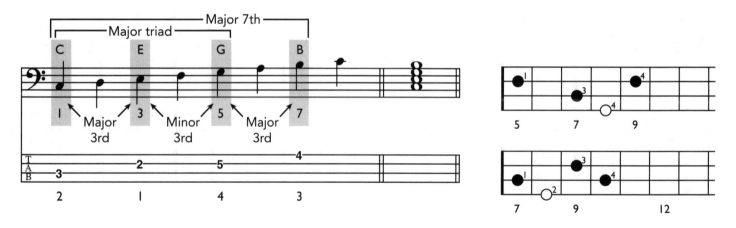

Dominant 7th

A *dominant 7th chord* is constructed by taking a major triad, or 1st, 3rd, and 5th of a major scale, and adding a minor 7th interval above the root. The resulting scale degrees are 1, 3, 5, and ♭7. The intervals are major 3rd–minor 3rd–minor 3rd.

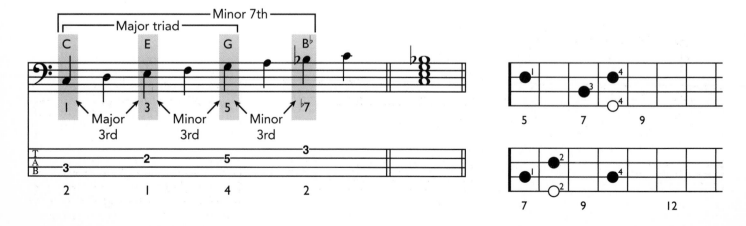

Minor 7th

A *minor 7th chord* is constructed by taking a minor triad, or 1st, ♭3rd, and 5th of a major scale, and adding a minor 7th interval above the root. The resulting scale degrees are 1, ♭3, 5, and ♭7. The intervals are minor 3rd–major 3rd–minor 3rd.

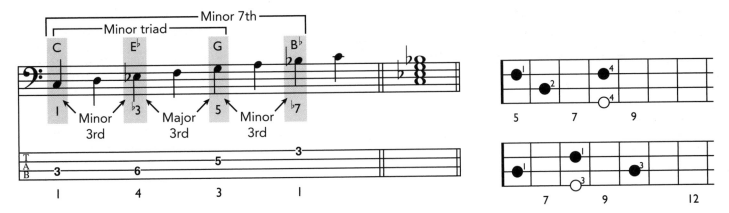

Minor 7♭5 (Half Diminished)

A *minor 7♭5 chord* (sometimes called a *half-diminished chord*) can be constructed by taking a diminished triad, or 1st, ♭3rd, and ♭5th scale degrees, and adding a minor 7th interval above the root. The resulting scale degrees are 1, ♭3, ♭5, and ♭7. The intervals are minor 3rd–minor 3rd–major 3rd.

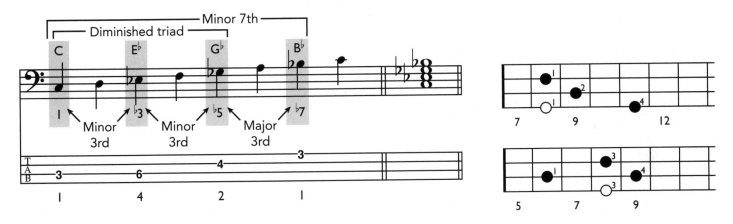

Diminished 7th

A *diminished 7th chord* can be constructed by taking a diminished triad, or 1st, ♭3rd, and ♭5th scale degrees, and adding a diminished 7th interval (equivalent to a major 6th) above the root. The resulting scale degrees are 1, ♭3, ♭5, and ♭♭7. The intervals are minor 3rd–minor 3rd–minor 3rd.

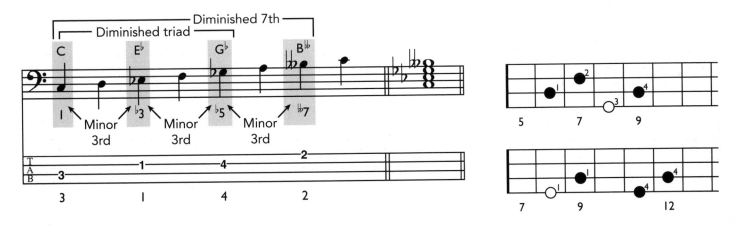

Diatonic Harmony

Diatonic means "in the key." *Harmony* is the simultaneous sounding of multiple tones to form chords. So, *diatonic harmony* means "chords within the key." Stacking diatonic 3rds on each note of the major scale—two 3rds to create triads and three 3rds to create 7th chords—creates diatonic chords of a major key or scale.

It is important for any bassist to be able to play the harmony of all 12 major scales. This will help enable you to create bass lines comfortably in every key. Following is the diatonic harmony for triads and 7th chords.

Diatonic Triads

Below are triads built on each degree of the major scale. Remember that triads consist of three notes, each separated by an interval of a 3rd.

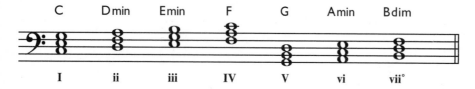

The Roman numerals below the staff indicate the scale degrees on which each triad is constructed. Upper-case Roman numerals are used for the major triads, I, IV, and V. Lower-case Roman numerals are used for the minor triads, ii, iii, and vi. The vii° triad is diminished. This is true in every major key. In other keys, the quality of each chord remains the same, but the notes change.

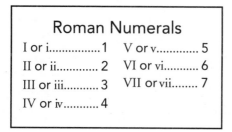

Diatonic 7th Chords

Shown here are 7th chords built on each degree of the major scale. Notice that all 7th chords have four notes, each separated by a 3rd.

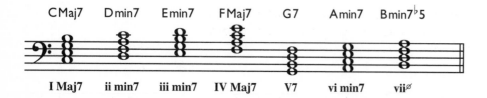

As with diatonic triads, the *quality* of diatonic 7th chords remains the same in every key; only the notes change.

Chord Chart

Here is a chord chart that includes triads, 7th chords, and a few other chord types you may encounter. In the left-hand column, you will find the chord symbol used to indicate that particular chord. In the center column, you will find an example using the note C as the root of the chord. In the right-hand column, you will find the scale degrees that create the chord. Try to become familiar with all of the chord types shown.

MAJOR CHORDS	Note Names	Scale Degrees
C	C–E–G	1–3–5
C6	C–E–G–A	1–3–5–6
CMaj7	C–E–G–B	1–3–5–7
CMaj7♯11	C–E–G–B–F♯	1–3–5–7–♯11
CAug	C–E–G♯	1–3–♯5
DOMINANT CHORDS	**Note Names**	**Scale Degrees**
C7	C–E–G–B♭	1–3–5–♭7
C7♭9	C–E–G–B♭–D♭	1–3–5–♭7–♭9
C7+ (has ♯5, ♯11)	C–E–G♯–B♭–F♯	1–3–♯5–♭7–♯11
C7+9 (has ♯5, ♭9, ♯11)	C–E–G♯–B♭–D♭–F♯	1–3–♯5–♭7–♭9–♯11
C7♯11	C–E–G–B♭–D–F♯	1–3–5–♭7–9–♯11
C7sus4	C–F–G–B♭	1–4–5–♭7
MINOR CHORDS	**Note Names**	**Scale Degrees**
Cmin	C–E♭–G	1–♭3–5
Cmin6	C–E♭–G–A	1–♭3–5–6
Cmin7	C–E♭–G–B♭	1–♭3–5–♭7
Cmin7♭5	C–E♭–G♭–B♭	1–♭3–♭5–♭7
Cmin(Maj7)	C–E♭–G–B	1–♭3–5–7
HALF DIMINISHED	**Note Names**	**Scale Degrees**
C⌀7 or Cmin7♭5	C–E♭–G♭–B♭	1–♭3–♭5–♭7
DIMINISHED	**Note Names**	**Scale Degrees**
C°7	C–E♭–G♭–B♭♭ (A)	1–♭3–♭5–♭♭7

Unfortunately, chord symbols are not standardized. The chord symbols above are the ones used in this book, but a versatile bassist should be familiar with common variations of these chord symbols. Here's a list of some variations you might see:

- **Major:** Maj, M, △
- **Dominant:** 7, dom7
- **Minor:** min, mi, m, -
- **Diminished:** °, dim
- **Augmented:** Aug, +

Although there are other chords you may come across, this list gives you a good start on the chord qualities you will most often encounter when reading chord changes.

CHAPTER FIVE
MODES AND SCALES

+++

Modes of the Major Scale

A *mode* is created by starting a scale on a note other than its root. Technically, all scales have their own sets of modes, but usually when people say "modes," they mean the seven modes of the major scale. The first mode is the *Ionian* mode, which is the same as the major scale. The second mode, *Dorian*, is created by starting on the 2nd note of the major scale and playing up one octave from that point. The third mode, *Phrygian*, starts on the 3rd note of the major scale, and so on.

Following are the modes of the C Major scale and some fingering options for each (shown to the right). These fingerings are based on *tetrachords*, four-note patterns that you can learn more about in *Beginning Electric Bass* (#22910). An arrow ⟶ indicates a shift of your left-hand position.

Ionian

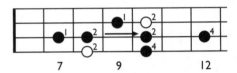
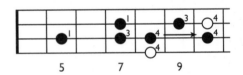

Dorian

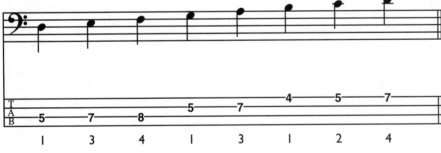
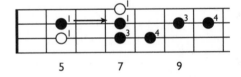
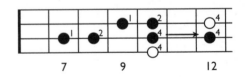

Phrygian

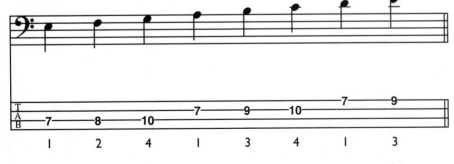
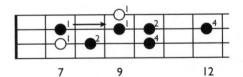
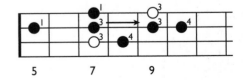

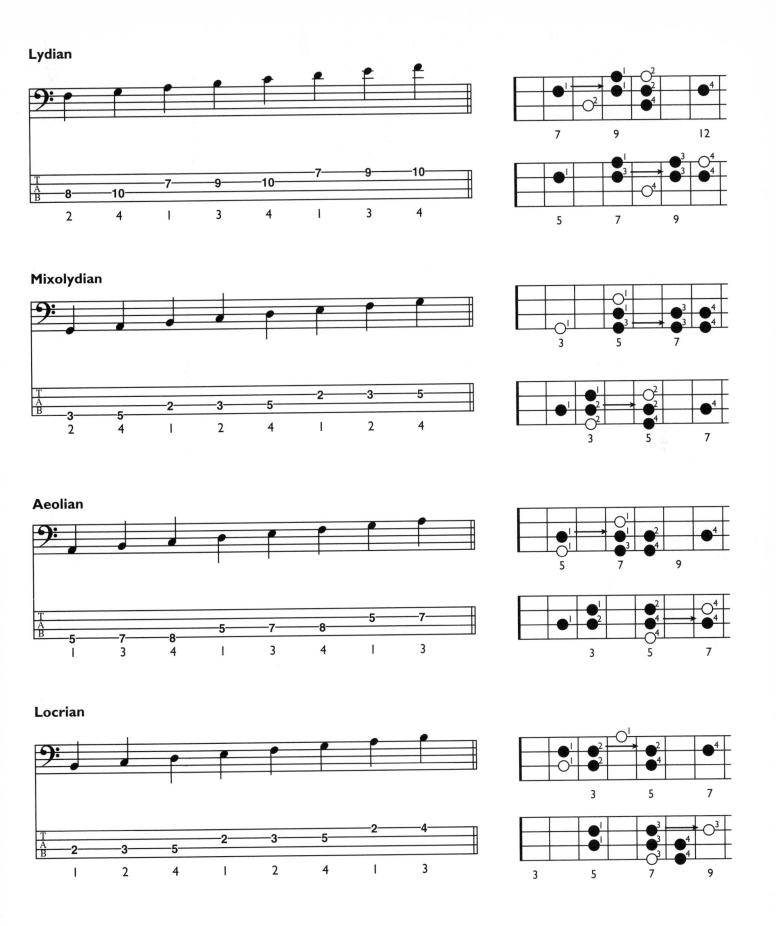

After you get the modes of the C Major scale under your fingers, try playing through
the modes of other major keys.

Minor Scales

For every major scale, there is a minor scale with the exact same notes and key signature. This is called the *relative minor* or *natural minor scale*. The relative minor scale can be found by starting on the 6th degree of the major scale and playing to its octave; in other words, it is identical to the Aeolian mode (see page 17). For example, if we play a C Major scale starting on the 6th degree (A) and play to the octave (A), we have played an A Natural Minor scale. The chart on page 10 shows the relative minor for each major key. The distinguishing degrees of the minor scale are ♭3, ♭6, and ♭7. All natural minor scales are built using the formula 1–2–♭3–4–5–♭6–♭7.

There are three forms of the minor scale. In addition to the natural minor scale, there are also the *harmonic minor* and *melodic minor* scales. The harmonic minor scale differs from the natural minor scale in that it has a natural (not flatted) 7th. It's spelled 1–2–♭3–4–5–♭6–7. The melodic minor scale is different, with a natural 6th and 7th: 1–2–♭3–4–5–6–7.

Here are the three forms of the minor scale. The TAB shows a suggested fingering for each scale, which is also shown to the right in scale diagram form. The distinguishing tones of each scale are highlighted.

C Natural Minor Scale

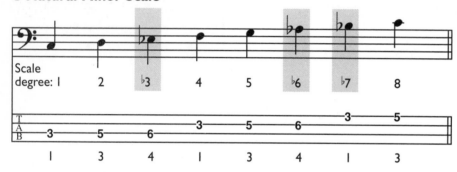
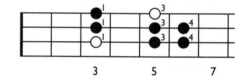

C Harmonic Minor Scale

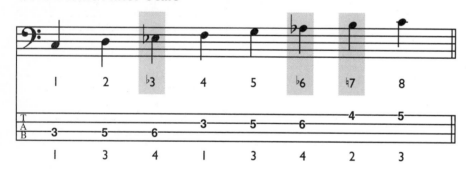
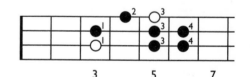

C Melodic Minor Scale

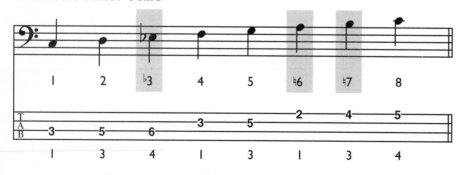
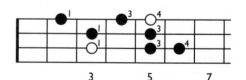

Pentatonic and Blues Scales

A *pentatonic scale* consists of five notes. The most commonly used pentatonic scales are the *major pentatonic* and the *minor pentatonic*. These scales make up a large part of the melodic vocabulary for rock, blues, country, and even jazz styles. Let's look at both of these pentatonic scales.

Major Pentatonic Scales

The major pentatonic scale consists of scale degrees 1, 2, 3, 5, and 6. It is similar to the major scale, but with scale degrees 4 and 7 omitted. This is a "bright" or "cheerful" sounding scale. It is often used in rock, country, and blues.

Here is a C Major Pentatonic scale with two common fingerings.

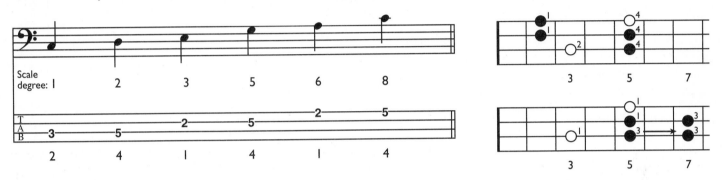

Minor Pentatonic Scales

The minor pentatonic consists of scale degrees 1, 3, 4, 5, and 7. This scale has a "darker" sound. It is one of the first scales learned by rock players and is also often used in blues and jazz.

Here are two common fingerings for the minor pentatonic scale.

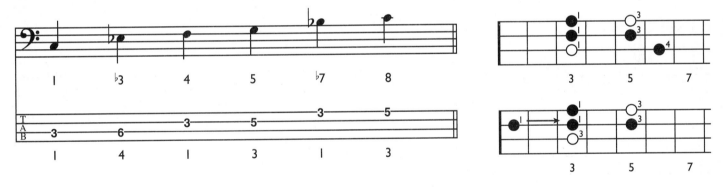

Blues Scale

The blues scale consists of the scale degrees 1, ♭3, 4, ♭5, 5, and ♭7. The ♭3, ♭5, and ♭7 scale degrees are known as *blue notes* and contribute to the "bluesy" sound of the scale. This scale is frequently used in all types of blues-influenced music.

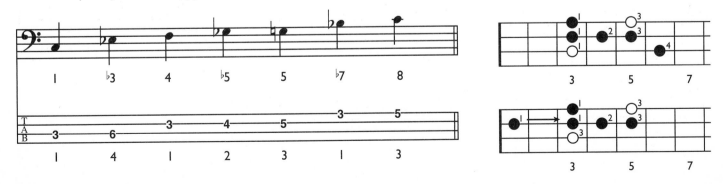

Diminished and Whole Tone Scales

Diminished and *whole tone* scales are used extensively for jazz improvisation. These scales are unique because they are *symmetrical*, meaning the interval pattern of each scale repeats itself. There are two different diminished scales we will look at, which are shown below.

Whole Step/Half Step Diminished

The *whole step/half step diminished scale* repeats a pattern of whole step–half step from the root of the scale to its octave. This scale can be played over diminished chords or can be played over dominant chords by starting the scale a half step above the root of the chord. For example, over a C7 chord, play a D♭ whole step/half step diminished scale.

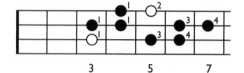

Half Step/Whole Step Diminished

The *half step/whole step diminished scale* repeats a pattern of half step–whole step from the root of the scale to its octave. This scale is often played over dominant 7th chords starting the scale on the root of the dominant 7th chord. For example, over a G7 chord, play a G half step/whole step diminished scale.

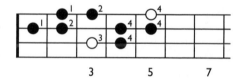

Whole Tone Scale

A whole tone scale repeats a pattern of whole steps from the root of the scale to its octave. This scale is often played over dominant 7th chords. For example, over a B♭7 chord, play a B♭ whole tone scale.

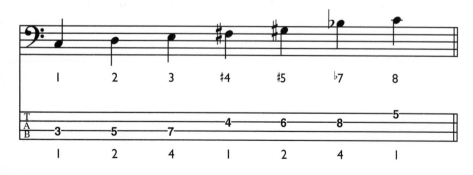
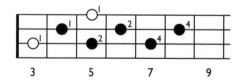

Scale Chart

When you are reading chord symbols and trying to create a bass line, it is helpful to know which scales are commonly used with which chords. The scale chart below shows you the scales most often used for various chord types. Think of them as suggestions. In some situations, you might have several scale choices.

Care should be taken to avoid scale degrees that clash with the chord tones. These notes should be used sparingly. A good example is playing the 4th over a major chord. Because the 4th is a half step higher than the major 3rd of the chord, it creates an unpleasant sound and should only be used in passing.

MAJOR CHORDS	Scale Name	Scale in the Key of C
C	Major Pentatonic	C–D–E–G–A–C
C6	Major Pentatonic	C–D–E–G–A–C
C	Major (don't emphasize 4th)	C–D–E–F–G–A–B–C
C♯11	Lydian	C–D–E–F♯–G–A–B–C
CAug	Lydian Augmented	C–D–E–F♯–G♯–A–B–C

DOMINANT CHORDS	Scale Name	Scale in the Key of C
C7	Mixolydian (don't emphasize 4th)	C–D–E–F–G–A–B♭–C
C7♭9	Diminished (half step/whole step)	C–D♭–E♭–E–F♯–G–A–B♭–C
C7+9 (also has ♯5, ♭9, ♯11)	Diminished Whole Tone	C–D♭–D♯–E–F♯–G♯–B♭–C
C7+ (has ♯5, ♯11)	Whole Tone	C–D–E–F♯–G♯–B♭
C7♯11	Lydian ♭7	C–D–E–F♯–G–A–B♭–C
C7 sus4	Mixolydian (don't emphasize 3rd)	C–D–E–F–G–A–B♭–C

MINOR CHORDS	Scale Name	Scale in the Key of C
Cmin	Minor Pentatonic	C–E♭–F–G–B♭–C
Cmin♭6	Natural Minor	C–D–E♭–F–G–A♭–B♭–C
Cmin7	Dorian	C–D–E♭–F–G–A–B♭–C
Cmin	Melodic Minor	C–D–E♭–F–G–A–B–C

HALF DIMINISHED	Scale Name	Scale in the Key of C
C⌀7 or Cmin7♭5	Locrian	C–D♭–E♭–F–G♭–A♭–B♭–C

DIMINISHED	Scale Name	Scale in the Key of C
C°7	Diminished (whole step/half step)	C–D–E♭–F–G♭–A♭–A–B–C

CHAPTER SIX
THE BLUES

+ +

Early blues was born in the Mississippi Delta, hence the name *delta blues*. The blues traveled to other states such as Texas, Tennessee, and eventually Illinois. When the blues arrived in Chicago, there was a significant change in the music as musicians adopted the electric guitar and electric bass. The music became louder, bass players could be heard, and groups now typically included drummers. The result of these developments was the birth of what we now call *urban blues*.

As the premier bassist and pre-eminent songwriter of his era, Willie Dixon was a towering figure in the history and creation of Chicago blues. Dixon wrote over 500 songs and played bass on sessions for Chuck Berry, Muddy Waters, and Howlin' Wolf. Another legendary blues bassist is Donald "Duck" Dunn. Dunn played with many great blues and R&B artists including Wilson Pickett, Albert King, Booker T. & the MG's, Freddie King, and many others. Some may know him best for his work with The Blues Brothers.

Modern bassists have carried on the tradition of blues bass, and some have added the use of modern techniques to enhance the bass line. Roscoe Beck, who is known for his work with guitarists Robben Ford and Eric Johnson, is a great player in his own right.

The Blues Form

Blues bass lines are often comprised of one- or two-bar bass patterns that are repeated throughout the duration of the *form*, or structure. The most commonly used blues form is the *12-bar blues*. The harmonic structure of the blues is basically made up of the I, IV, and V chords. (For a review of I, IV, and V chords, refer to diatonic harmony on page 14.) Shown below is a 12-bar blues song form in A Major. This type of notation is called *slash notation*. It doesn't tell you which notes to play; it just shows the chord changes so that you can create your own bass line. Notice that the I, IV, and V chords (A7, D7, and E7) are all dominant 7th chords. Dominant 7th chords are the norm in blues music.

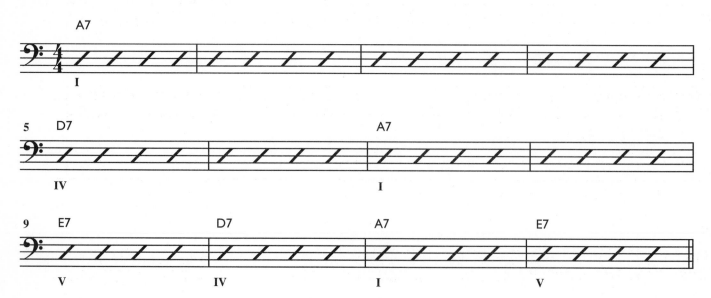

The Quick Four

Many blues tunes add the IV chord in bar 2. This variation is known as a *quick four*.

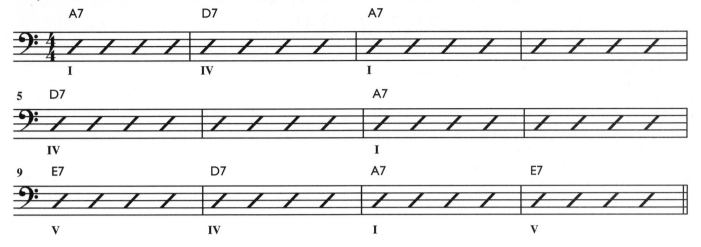

Turnarounds

Many blues form variations can be found in the *turnaround,* or the last four bars of the progression. Below are four frequently used turnarounds in the 12-bar blues. Turnaround D is typical of a jazzy blues such as the tune "Route 66."

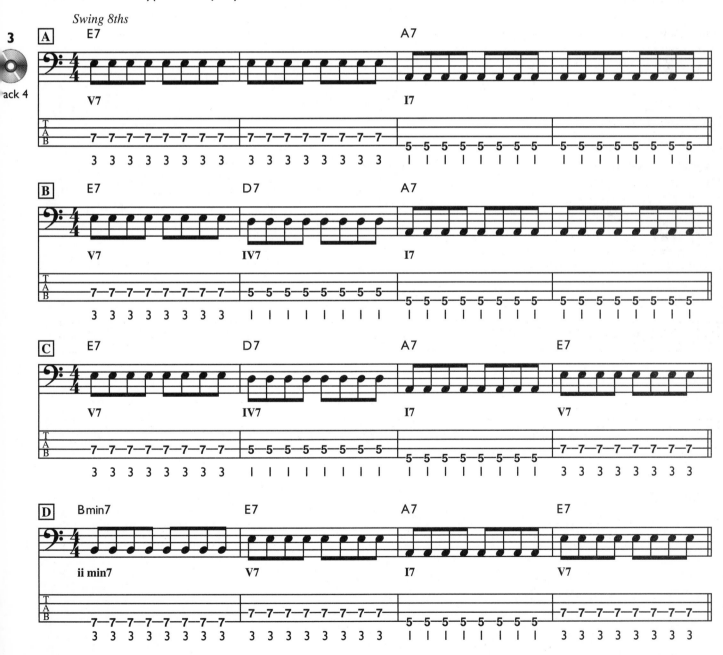

Major Pentatonic Blues

The blues is probably the most commonly used song form in American music, crossing the boundaries of style. The *blues progression*, more particularly the 12-bar blues, and the I–IV–V chord progression that is its foundation, is used in the styles of rockabilly, country, classic rock, hard rock, reggae, punk rock, folk, and many other styles of music.

In traditional blues, dominant 7th chords are often used in the chord progressions. In rock music that uses the 12-bar blues progression, major chords are commonly used. As we know from the scale chart (page 21) the major pentatonic scale is often used to create bass lines over major chords. (To review the major pentatonic scale, refer to page 19.)

Below are popular patterns derived from the major pentatonic scale that can be used for blues bass lines. These one- and two-bar patterns can be used on different variations of the blues progression. When the duration of a chord is one bar, you can use the one-bar patterns, and when the duration of a chord is two bars, you have the option of playing two one-bar patterns or using a two-bar pattern. On the CD, the one-bar examples are repeated four times, and the two-bar examples are repeated two times.

After you get all of these patterns under your fingers, play each one throughout the duration of the blues progression, and then experiment with mixing up the patterns to create variety in your bass lines.

One-Bar Major Pentatonic Patterns

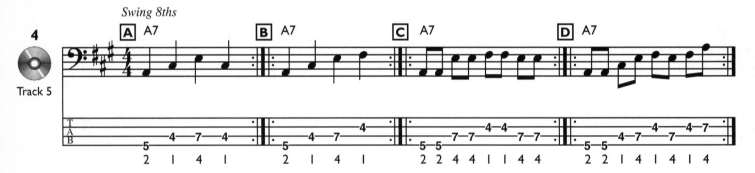

Two-Bar Major Pentatonic Patterns

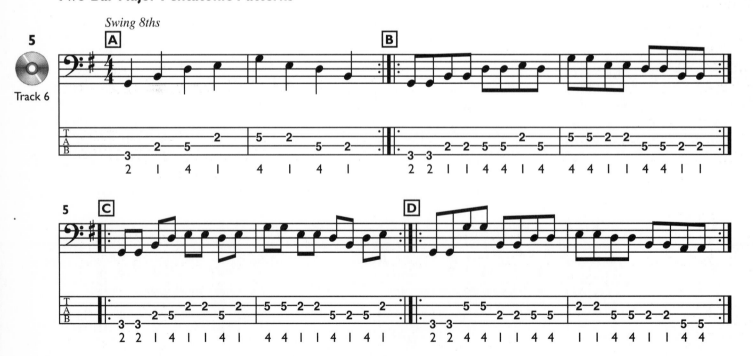

Bass Patterns for Dominant 7th Blues

When using the dominant 7th chord in blues progressions, the harmony sounds more "bluesy" than when using major chords. Dominant 7th chords consist of chord tones 1, 3, 5, and ♭7. The major 3rd and the minor 7th form the interval of a diminished 5th or *tritone*, which contributes to the unique sound of the blues in that the I, IV, and V chords are all dominant 7th chords. The scale we often use to create bass lines over the dominant 7th chord is the Mixolydian mode (refer to page 17). The bass patterns below can be played over dominant 7th chords. Some patterns use chord tones exclusively, while others incorporate tones from the Mixolydian scale. The one-bar patterns repeat four times, and the two-bar patterns two times. All of these patterns are written in C, but once you have them under your fingers, try playing them in all 12 keys.

One-Bar Dominant 7th Patterns

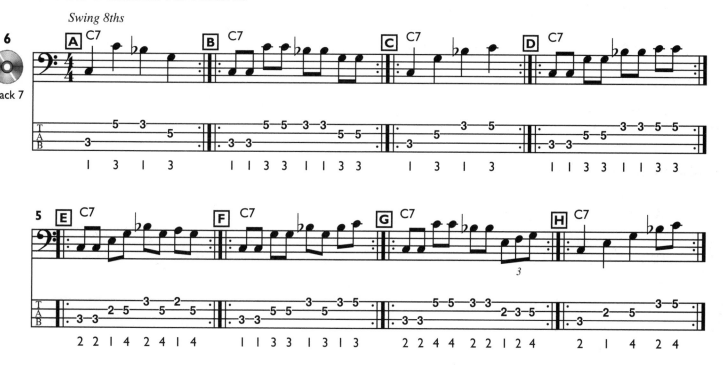

Two-Bar Dominant 7th Patterns

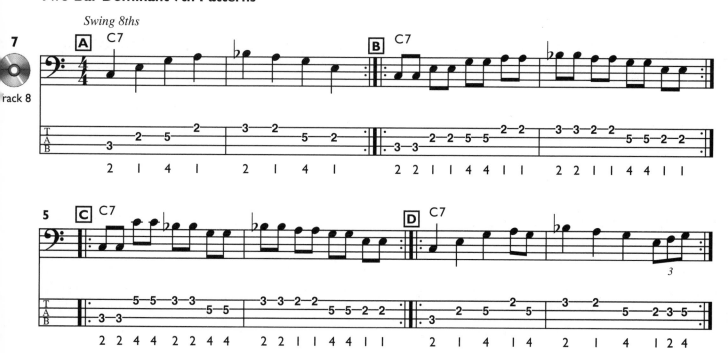

Minor Pentatonic and Blues Scale Bass Patterns

The minor pentatonic and blues scales, along with the major pentatonic scale, make up the basic vocabulary for blues guitarists. When creating bass lines over dominant 7th chords, bassists usually outline the chord sound by incorporating chord tones and notes from the Mixolydian mode. Because the minor pentatonic and blues scales contain the minor 3rd scale degree, using them to create a bass part over a dominant 7th chord would lead to the minor 3rd clashing with the major 3rd from the chord. Therefore, the minor pentatonic and blues scales are not commonly used for creating bass lines over dominant 7th chords, but are excellent for playing over minor chords, "5" chords (see page 38), and riff-oriented tunes. These scales are also the staple for melodic material and soloing over the blues. The one-bar patterns repeat four times, and the two-bar patterns repeat two times.

One-Bar Patterns Derived from the Minor Pentatonic Scale

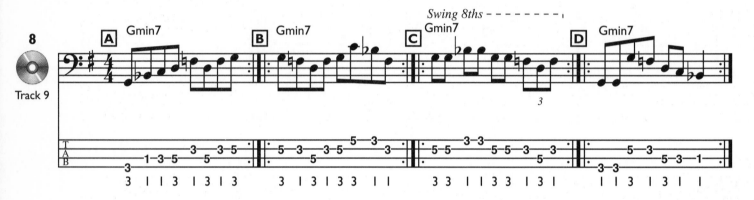

Two-Bar Patterns Derived from the Minor Pentatonic Scale

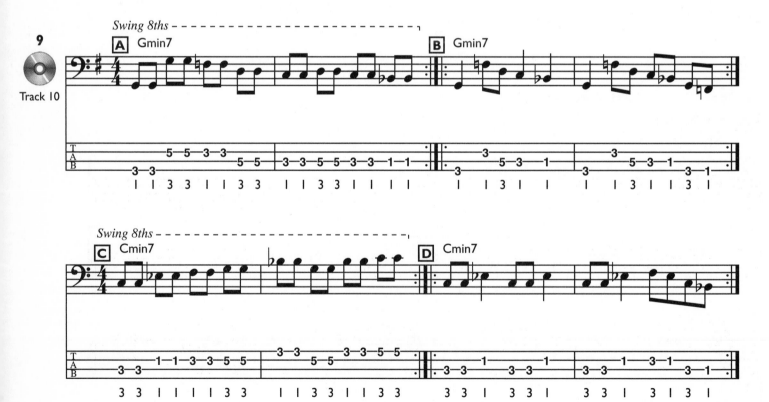

Blues Scale Riffs

As with the minor pentatonic scale, the blues scale can be used by bass players over minor chords, 5 chords, or in riff-oriented tunes. The blues scale is also used extensively for soloing over the blues. It is essential for any rock or blues bassist to get the blues scale under their fingers in the early stages of their development, as it will be used extensively in the rock and blues genres. Below are one- and two-bar blues scale bass patterns. The one-bar riffs are played four times, and the two-bar riffs are played two times. Also, notice that examples 10A and 10C make use of the *hammer-on* technique. This means you "hammer" your 3rd finger onto the 7th fret to play the E♮, without plucking with your right hand.

$\underset{\text{H}}{\frown}$ = Hammer-on

One-Bar Blues Scale Riffs

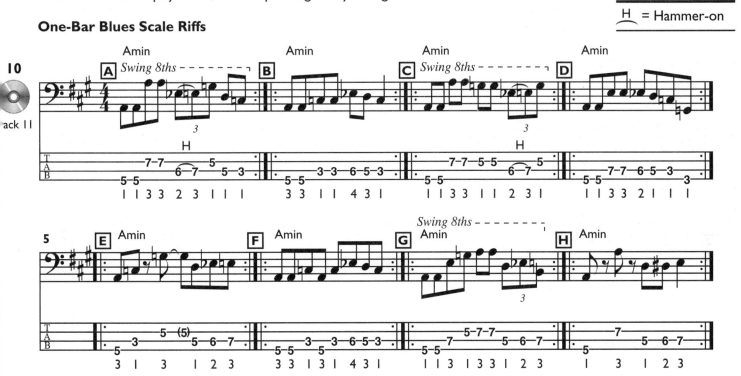

Two-Bar Blues Scale Riffs

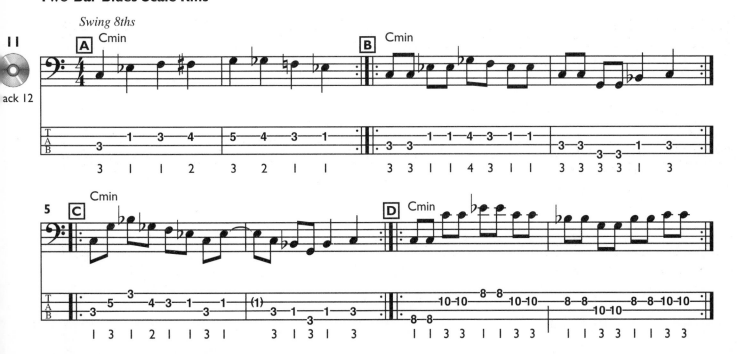

$\frac{12}{8}$ Slow Blues

Slow-tempo blues songs are often written using the $\frac{12}{8}$ time signature, which feels like four beats, each subdivided into three parts: **1**–2–3–**2**–2–3–**3**–2–3–**4**–2–3. The following example shows how the exact same pattern can be written using either $\frac{12}{8}$ or $\frac{4}{4}$.

Generations of blues musicians have discovered that counting in $\frac{12}{8}$ helps them play slow tempos more accurately. Playing in $\frac{4}{4}$, there is a natural tendency to rush the beat, whereas in $\frac{12}{8}$, a slow tempo sounds quite natural and powerful. Check out the $\frac{12}{8}$ slow blues shown below. The I7–IV7–I7–V7 turnaround is typical of a slow blues.

Slow Blues in $\frac{12}{8}$

CHAPTER SEVEN
ROCKABILLY

++

Rockabilly was born in the 1950s as a blend of blues, country, and gospel. There was a lot of overlap between rockabilly and early rock 'n' roll. Rockabilly had a stronger country influence than the rock 'n' roll that came later. Artists such as Elvis Presley, Johnny Cash, Jerry Lee Lewis, Chuck Berry, and Bill Haley & His Comets were some of many artists to inspire youngsters with the rockabilly sound.

In the late 1970s and early '80s, the Stray Cats led a rockabilly revival and helped revive the sound. Check out the tunes "Rock This Town" and "Stray Cat Strut" to hear the simple yet hip sound of rockabilly.

Rockabilly bass lines are often similar to blues bass lines. The difference is mostly in feel; rockabilly has an obvious country music influence, and the drummer typically plays a strong *backbeat* on the snare drum (beats 2 and 4). Bass lines are typically played on acoustic upright bass, with the bassist using the slap style for a percussive sound.

The bass line below can be heard on tunes like "Blue Suede Shoes."

 ## Aqua Leather Boots

Track 15

This rockabilly bass line is in the style of the tune "Shake, Rattle, and Roll," as recorded by Bill Haley & His Comets. The figure in bars 11 and 12 is commonly found in rockabilly and blues styles. It uses a hammer-on (see page 27) of the 1st finger onto the 1st fret. Note that there are a couple of passages in the walking bass style (see page 78) using notes of the E Mixolydian scale.

Jingle, Quake, and Sway

Track 16

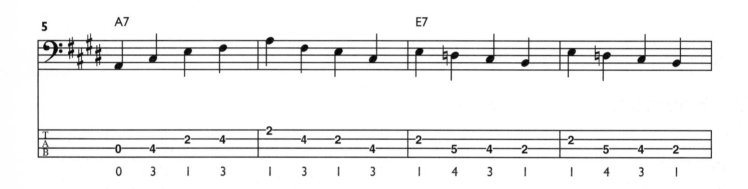

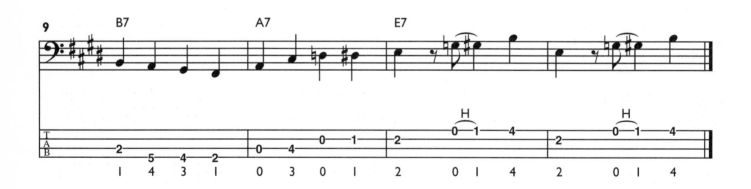

This line is in the style of the Jerry Lee Lewis recording of "Great Balls of Fire."

Huge Spheres of Flame

Track 17

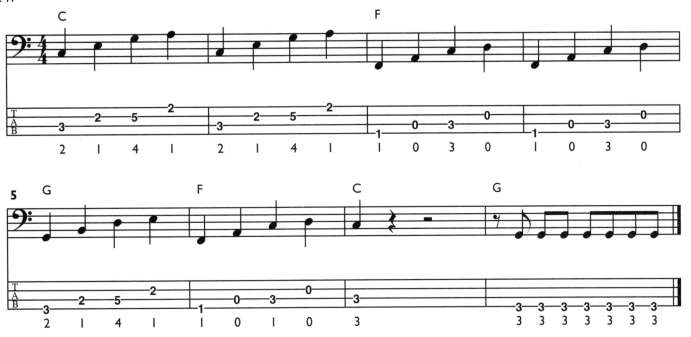

This bass line is in the style of tunes by Chuck Berry such as "Johnny B. Goode" and "Reelin' and Rockin'." Chuck Berry's style was somewhere between rockabilly and early rock 'n' roll.

Reeled and Rocked

Track 18

Country Bass Lines

Country music appears in this chapter because it is a close relative of rockabilly. Its roots are in folk, Appalachian, and hillbilly music. Country music as a whole had a profound impact on the American subconscious and provided the United States with cultural identity. The performers, audience, and stories were American. From a musical standpoint, the music emphasized first the story, then the singer, then the musical arrangement. The bass lines in country music are, for the most part, simple, but effective. A typical country bass part consists of the root and 5th on beats 1 and 3 of the measure, with occasional passing tone passages. Country music is also commonly written and played in *cut time* ¢ feel (see page 50). Shown below is an example of a bass line in the style of a more traditional country style than the more "rocked out" rockabilly style.

 # Blues for the Country

Track 19

CHAPTER EIGHT
ROCK BASS LINES

+++

What is rock music? The precursor to rock music was the blues. The evolution of rock has taken us from the early rockabilly/rock 'n' roll music of Elvis Presley in the 1950s to the many artists who helped the music evolve to the present day. The early "supergroups" were largely influenced by rhythm and blues, a prime example being Led Zeppelin, whose bassist John Paul Jones gave us plenty of great bass lines to listen to and learn. The band Cream, with guitarist Eric Clapton and bassist Jack Bruce, was one of the first groups to take extended jams on their tunes when playing live concerts, and Jack Bruce was one of the first to warrant the term "lead bass" as he took bass solos and played melodically during the extended jams. Noel Redding and Billy Cox, both bassists for Jimi Hendrix, gave us some great driving rock bass lines. Paul McCartney of The Beatles gave us some of the most musical and melodic rock bass lines ever played. These legends paved the way for great players such as Chris Squire of Yes, who played great melodic bass lines with the incredible tone of his Rickenbacker bass.

The 1970s, 1980s, and 1990s brought many other sub-genres of rock music, including alternative rock, glamour rock, heavy metal, punk rock, pop rock, and many other styles of rock music. From the heavy bass lines of Black Sabbath's Geezer Butler, to the simple but very effective bass lines of Sting in the band the Police, there are many genres of rock music and bassists who deserve mention.

Let's look at bass lines in some of the more popular—and perhaps more interesting—bass-oriented rock styles that exist. Get these under your fingers and enjoy!

Classic Rock

How is classic rock different from the "oldies?" Classic rock grew out of a radio format known as *Album-Oriented Rock* (AOR). AOR focuses on entire albums, whereas the oldies genre encompasses selected singles that found commercial success. The heyday of classic rock came in the 1960s and 1970s with supergroups such as The Beatles, The Rolling Stones, Led Zeppelin, Cream, Jimi Hendrix, and The Yardbirds.

Since the blues played a major role in the development of rock music, many classic rock groups were rooted in the blues. When you listen to Led Zeppelin, you can hear the blues forms and blues influence in their music. The same goes for Cream, Clapton, Hendrix, The Rolling Stones, and many others. Below are a couple of bass lines that are in the styles of blues-rooted, classic-rock bass lines.

Jack Bruce of Cream

These bass lines are in the style of Jack Bruce. Example 13A is in the style of "Sunshine of Your Love," 13B is in the style of "Crossroads," 13C is in the style of "White Room," and 13D is in the style of "Politician."

13 Track 20

This line is in the style of Jack Bruce playing the blues classic "Born Under a Bad Sign."

14 Track 21

John Paul Jones of Led Zeppelin

Another important and influential rock bassist was John Paul Jones of Led Zeppelin. Zeppelin was heavily influenced by the blues, but because of their loud and powerful sound, they are sometimes called the first "heavy metal" band. Of course, Led Zeppelin was perhaps mellow compared to some of the heavy metal bands that followed, and today are best remembered as a great classic rock 'n' roll band. Following are some bass lines in the style of John Paul Jones and Led Zeppelin.

This bass line is in the style of the classic Zeppelin tune "Moby Dick."

This bass line is in the style of the Zeppelin classic "Immigrant Song."

This one is in the style of "The Ocean."

This is in the style of "Heartbreaker."

John Entwistle of The Who

Another influential classic rock bassist was John Entwistle of The Who. You can hear Entwistle's unique right-hand plucking technique on classic tunes such as "My Generation" and "Pinball Wizard." Below are some bass lines in his style. Example 16A is in the style of "My Generation," and 16B is in the style of "Pinball Wizard."

Bill Wyman of The Rolling Stones

The Rolling Stones are one of the quintessential classic rock bands. Bill Wyman laid down some memorable bass lines, such the groove in "Jumpin' Jack Flash." The following is in the style of that song.

This riff is in the style of the Stones classic "(I Can't Get No) Satisfaction."

Paul McCartney of The Beatles

Considered by many to be the most influential rock band ever formed, The Beatles recorded a string of significant records and pumped out many hits. The Beatles took America by storm in 1964 in a phenomenon known as "Beatlemania." Paul McCartney contributed on two fronts, as half of the songwriting team Lennon/McCartney and as a very influential bassist. He was one of the first to play "melodic bass lines" that did more than simply keep time with the drummer. From *Sgt. Pepper's Lonely Hearts Club Band* to *Magical Mystery Tour* to the *White Album*, Paul McCartney and The Beatles developed a timeless library of music.

Following is a bass line in the style of "Come Together." Note the use of a long *slide*. To execute a slide, keep your left-hand finger pressed against the fretboard while sliding up or down the neck from one note to the next.

18

Track 25

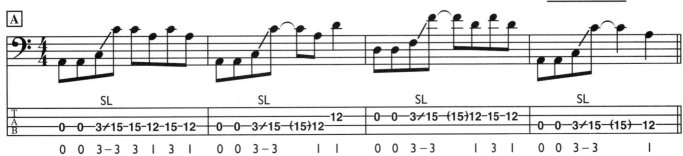

This one's in the style of "Day Tripper."

The following tune is in the style of "Birthday."

Hard Rock and Heavy Metal

Most hard rock and heavy metal songs are written around guitar parts that incorporate *5 chords*, also known as *power chords*. A 5 chord consists of the root and a perfect 5th. For example, a G5 chord consists of the notes G (the root) and D (the 5th). 5 chords became popular with the invention of the electric guitar. They sound best cranked up loud and played with lots of *distortion* (the "dirty" sound produced by overdriving an amplifier or using a distortion pedal effect). Since they have no 3rd, 5 chords are neither major nor minor. In the context of a rock song, the root and 5th alone achieve the desired "wall of sound" effect.

One foolproof strategy for hard rock bass is to lock in with the bass drum. The following groove is not rhythmically complex, but it is a perfect bass line for this style.

When the guitarist is playing 5 chords, most hard rock bassists rely not on harmonic complexity, but rather on fast, aggressive rhythms played at high volume. The rhythm of an eighth note and two sixteenths is often used in hard rock and heavy metal tunes for a "galloping" effect and sense of forward motion, as in the following example.

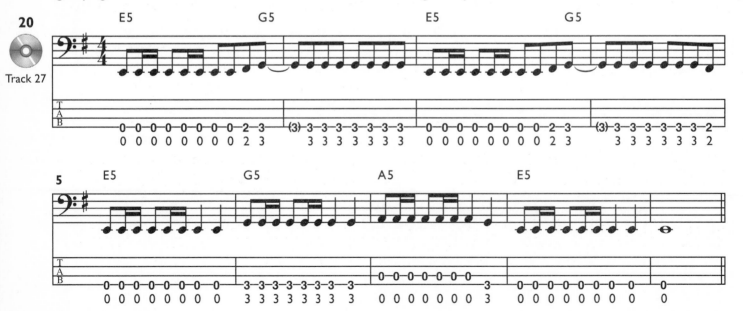

Let's examine just a few of the great heavy metal and hard rock bands and the bassists who created these inventive, signature bass lines.

Steve Harris of Iron Maiden

The first hard rock bassist we will check out is Steve Harris, the bassist for the great metal band Iron Maiden. The following bass line is in the style of "The Trooper." Notice the use of the eighth note/two sixteenth notes rhythm. This rhythm is found in many Steve Harris bass lines.

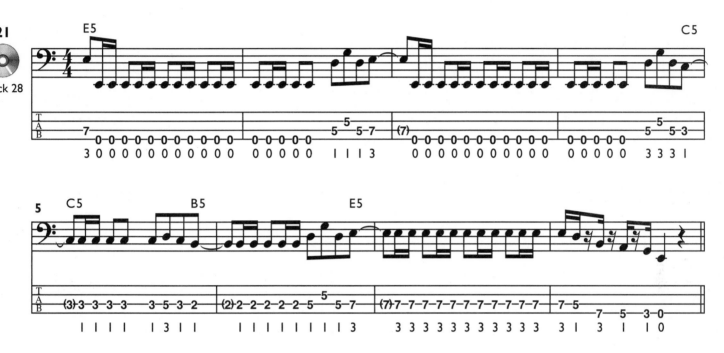

In the Iron Maiden tune "The Duelists," Steve Harris plays riffs using eighth-note triplets and quarter-note triplets. The eighth-note triplets, like the eighth note/two sixteenth note rhythm, gives the music a sort of "galloping" effect.

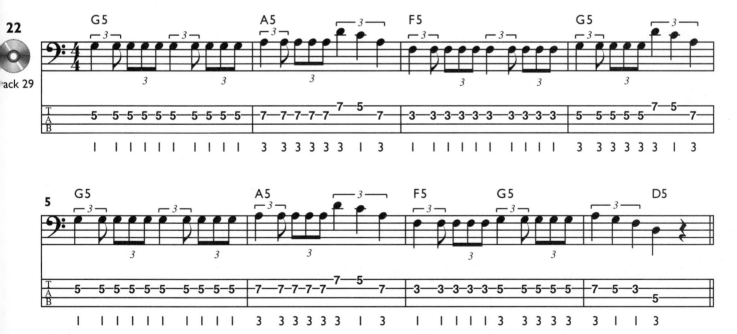

Geezer Butler of Black Sabbath

The name Black Sabbath is synonymous with heavy metal music. For a good introduction to bassist Geezer Butler's incredible riffing, check out their album *Paranoid*, which includes the heavy metal anthems "Iron Man," "War Pigs," and "Paranoid." When guitarist Tony Iommi joined Black Sabbath, Geezer began to tune his bass down from standard tuning EADG to C#F#BE. The result was less string tension and a darker sound. Nowadays, it is common for bassists to tune down a half step or whole step from standard tuning. Geezer took it even further by tuning down three half steps. Below are several bass lines in the style of Geezer Butler.

This bass line features a riff similar to one found in the Black Sabbath classic "Iron Man."

This bass line is also similar to a riff found in the tune "Iron Man." The notes are derived from the blues scale, and it sounds great when the guitarist is playing 5 chords.

This bass riff is also meant to be played over 5 chords and is similar to one found in the tune "Paranoid."

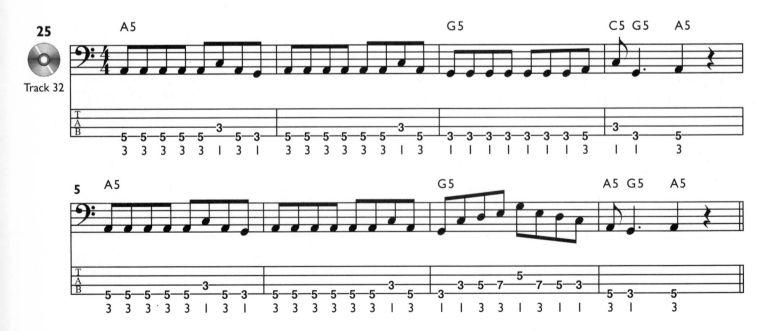

Cliff Williams of AC/DC

AC/DC is a hard rock band that formed in Australia in 1973. They are considered pioneers of the genre. The band is known for a hard and rough sound that has never been compromised through the years. Although the band is best known for the antics of lead guitarist Angus Young, they've featured some notable bassists as well. The band went through several bassists including George Young and Mark Evans, but Cliff Williams was the bassist on classic records such as *Powerage*, *Highway to Hell*, and *Back in Black*. Below are a few bass lines in the style of AC/DC as played by Cliff Williams.

This line is in the style of the classic "Back in Black."

Here is another groove in the style of Cliff Williams playing "Beating Around the Bush."

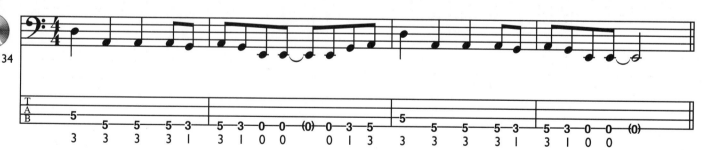

Heavy Metal Riff Using the Harmonic Minor Scale

Guitar players such as Randy Rhoads, Yngwie Malmsteen, Tony MacAlpine, and others expanded the vocabulary of heavy metal guitar by using the harmonic minor scale (see page 18). The harmonic minor scale provided darker, more exotic-sounding possibilities. The bass part below is derived from the D Harmonic Minor scale.

Harmonic Metal Minor

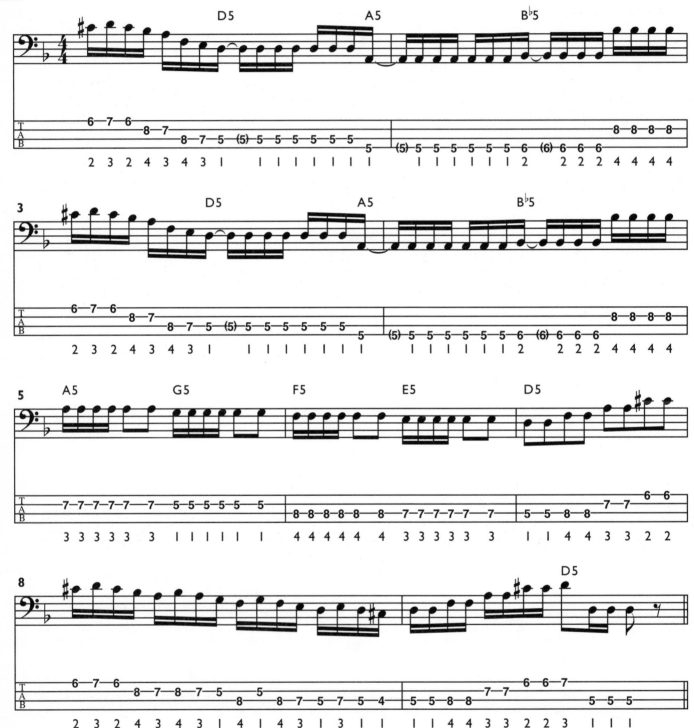

Progressive Rock

Progressive rock, also known as *prog rock* or *art rock*, is defined by its expansive song structures, ambitious lyrics, complex musicianship, and elaborate arrangements. Well-known progressive rock bands include Pink Floyd, Yes, Rush, and Emerson, Lake & Palmer.

Chris Squire of Yes

Chris Squire, bassist for Yes, created an original sound with his Rickenbacker bass and innovative use of effects and state-of-the-art amplification. His bass lines were melodic and imaginative, but he still knew how to lock in with the drummer and was fortunate to work with two of the best, Bill Bruford and Alan White.

Here is a bass line in the style of Chris Squire playing "Long Distance Runaround."

Here is another line in the style of Chris Squire on the Yes tune "Roundabout."

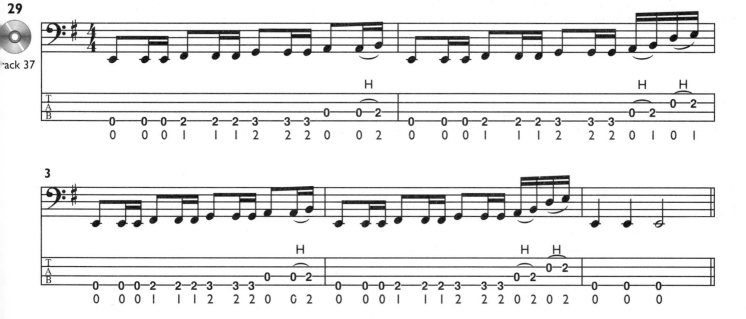

Geddy Lee of Rush

Rush formed in 1968 and quickly became known for their instrumental talents and complex compositions. The great bass playing and vocals of Geddy Lee powered the band. Their albums of the late 1970s featured complex and odd time signatures, as well as extended-length concept songs. Geddy's unique style and tone has influenced many up-and-coming bass players. Below are some bass lines in the style of Geddy Lee.

This one is in the style of his line on the tune "YYZ."

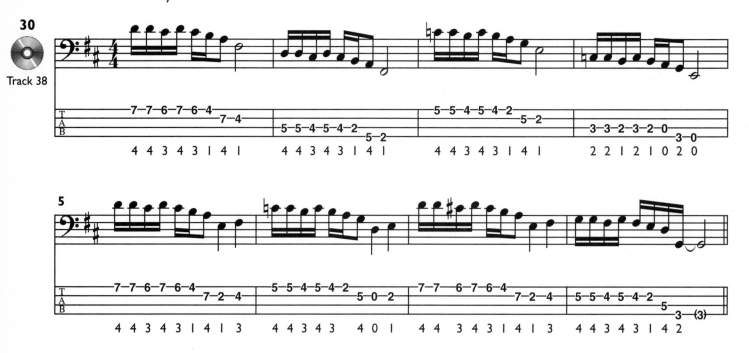

Here is another bass line in the style of Geddy Lee. Note the $\frac{7}{4}$ time signature, which means there are seven quarter-note beats per measure.

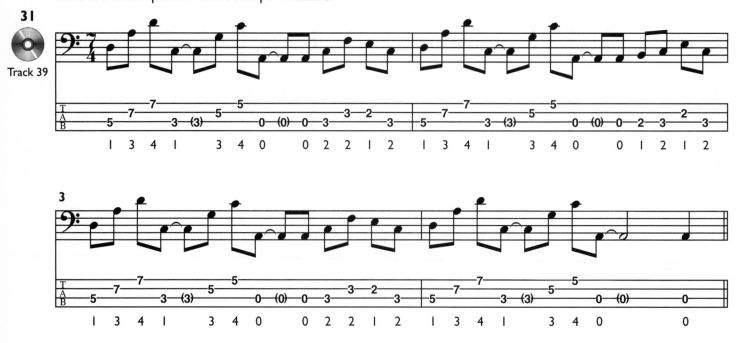

44   The Bass Style Resource

CHAPTER NINE
REGGAE/JAMAICAN MUSIC

+ +

Characteristics of Reggae Music

There are two styles of Jamaican music that have found their way into American popular music: reggae and ska. The origins of reggae lie in traditional African and Caribbean music, American rhythm & blues, and Jamaican ska. The characteristics of reggae music are its simplicity, relaxed yet insistent rhythms, and repetitive chord changes, usually in $\frac{4}{4}$ time. The bass plays a dominant role in reggae music. The appropriate bass sound is a thick and heavy tone with very little treble. The bass line is usually a simple repeated figure with very little harmonic movement. The guitar usually plays chords on beats 2 and 4 of each measure. It is common for the drums to emphasize the 3rd beat of the bar, a beat sometimes referred to as *one drop*. Sometimes the drums play on beats 1, 2, and 4, which is referred to as the *rockers* beat. In other cases, the bass drum plays on all four beats of the bar, which is referred to as the *steppers* beat. Keyboards and horns sometimes fill out the instrumentation in a reggae band, along with vocals.

Bob Marley and his band, The Wailers, are the most well-known reggae artists of all time. In the 1970s, reggae became a staple on radio stations around the world. Other popular reggae artists include Peter Tosh, Jimmy Cliff, and Sly and Robbie.

Aston Barrett was the primary bassist for Bob Marley and was responsible for most of the trademark bass lines on the popular Bob Marley classics. When you listen to classics like "Stir It Up," "I Shot the Sheriff," "No Woman, No Cry," or "One Love," you'll hear driving bass lines that almost hypnotize you.

Since reggae bass lines are not complex and seldom use advanced harmonies, you may notice the same bass lines in many reggae songs. As with bossa nova-style bass lines in Latin music, certain reggae bass lines can be found in a multitude of songs. You will find that bass lines often consist of one figure repeated for a long period of time. If you have put your audience into a trancelike state with your bass lines, you have done your job. The bass parts in reggae demand that you put aside your ego. They're all about the laid-back groove.

Some of the popular bands of the 1980s and beyond were influenced by Bob Marley and other reggae acts. One prominent rock band with an obvious reggae influence is the Police. Listen to the classic "Roxanne" for an example of the reggae influence.

On the following pages, we'll examine reggae grooves in the styles of Bob Marley and others.

Reggae Bass Lines

Aston Barrett of Bob Marley and The Wailers

Bob Marley was primarily responsible for reggae music's popularity in the United States. His songs and political activism helped him become well-known and helped reggae to flourish. Aston Barrett was not the only bassist to play with Bob Marley, but he did play on the most popular hits. Below are some reggae bass lines in the style of Aston Barrett. When playing these lines, remember to back off on the tone of your bass to cut the high frequencies of your sound. Also, boost the low end of your bass so you have a fat, thick bass tone.

This is in the style of Aston Barrett playing on the tune "Stir It Up."

This line is in the style of "I Shot the Sheriff."

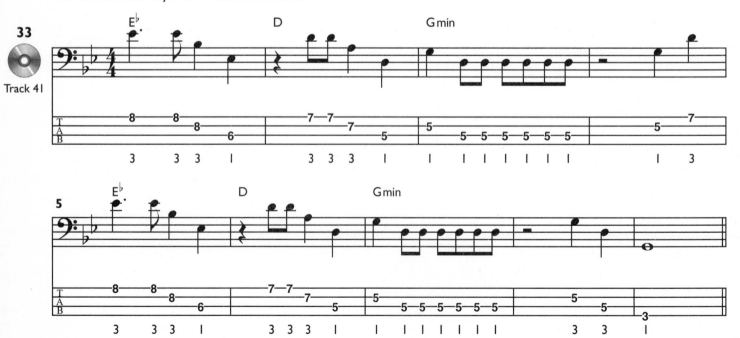

This bass line is in the style of Marley's classic "Get Up, Stand Up." The *quarter-note triplets* are the same idea as eighth-note triplets (page 6). Play three notes in the duration of two beats. Listen to the recording on the CD to get the right feeling.

$\quad\quad\quad$ = Quarter-note triplet

34

Track 42

This is in the style of Marley's "One Love."

35

Track 43

Here's one more bass line in the style of Aston Barrett's playing on the Bob Marley song "Jamming." Note the use of the quarter-note triplet in bar 8. This rhythm is often used in reggae bass lines.

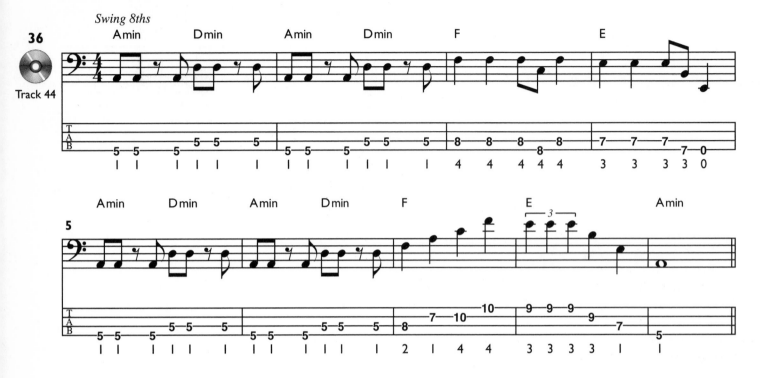

Peter Tosh

Peter Tosh was the guitarist in the original Wailers. After parting ways with Bob Marley, Tosh enjoyed success with albums such as 1976's *Legalize It*. He also contributed some bass playing to early Bob Marley records and probably did so on some of his own records.

The following example is in the style of the Peter Tosh tune "Equal Rights."

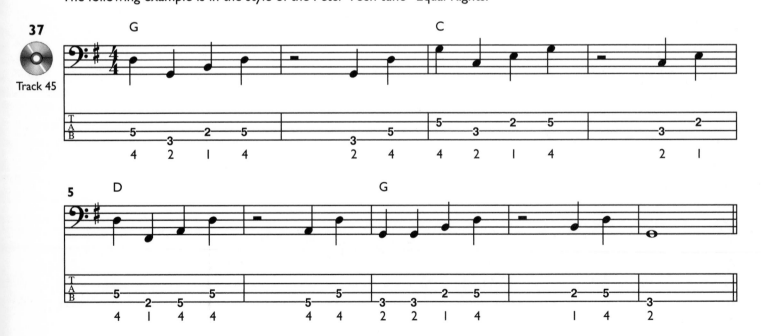

This one is in the style of another Peter Tosh tune.

38
ck 46

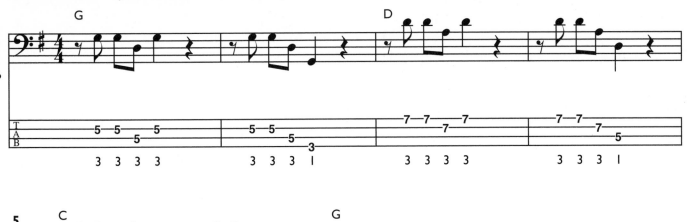

Check this one out. It's in the style of "Pick Myself Up."

39
ack 47

Ska

Ska music originated in Jamaica in the 1950s and was a precursor to reggae music. Early ska combined elements of Caribbean mento and calypso music, along with American jazz, and rhythm and blues. One of the most prominent bands of early ska was The Skatalites.

The second wave of ska hit the United Kingdom during the 1970s and '80s. Ska music of the UK revival is sometimes referred to as *2 Tone*, after the 2 Tone Records label. Through the influence of punk music, this brand of ska had faster tempos, fuller instrumentation, and a harder edge. Influential groups include the Beat (also known as the English Beat), The Selecter, and Madness.

The third wave of ska is sometimes referred to as *ska punk*. It was started by American musicians who were influenced by the 2 Tone bands. Important bands of the third wave include The Toasters, The Mighty Mighty Bosstones, and No Doubt.

The tempos in ska music are usually faster than those of reggae music. They are often felt in *cut time* (indicated by the ₵ symbol at the beginning of the staff). Cut time means each measure is counted in $\frac{2}{2}$ rather than $\frac{4}{4}$. In other words, each measure is counted as two half notes instead of four quarter notes.

The bass parts in ska tend to be busier than those in reggae, with less use of space and more use of walking bass (similar to the rockabilly style). Like reggae tunes, ska tunes tend to have simple chord progressions. The drumbeat is different in ska than in reggae. The drums in reggae often emphasize beat 3 with a bass drum kick, but in ska, beats 2 and 4 (a backbeat) are emphasized.

Vicky Rose and Matt Malles of The Toasters

Vicky Rose was the bassist in the original lineup of The Toasters. Matt Malles was the main bassist for the group throughout the 1990s. Both of these bassists contributed to the success of the group.

This bass line is in the style of The Toasters tune "2-Tone Army."

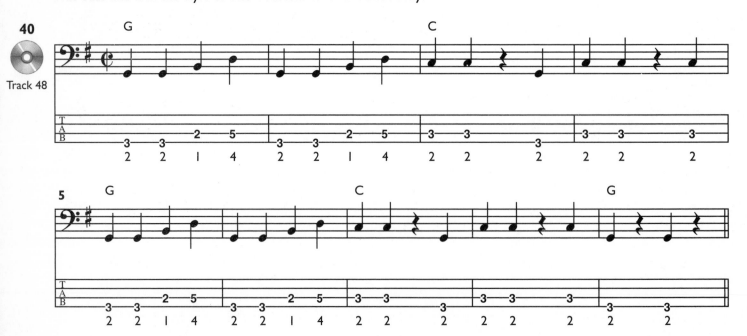

This bass line is also in the style of The Toasters and is similar to the one in the tune "Sweet Home Town Jamaica."

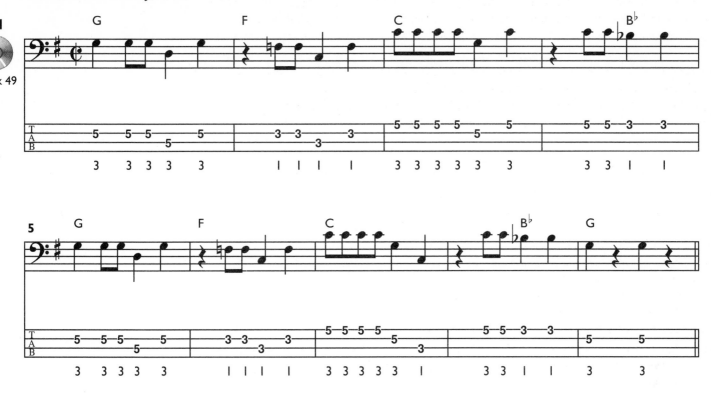

This bass line is derived from a two-chord progression and is in the style of The Toasters tune "New York Fever."

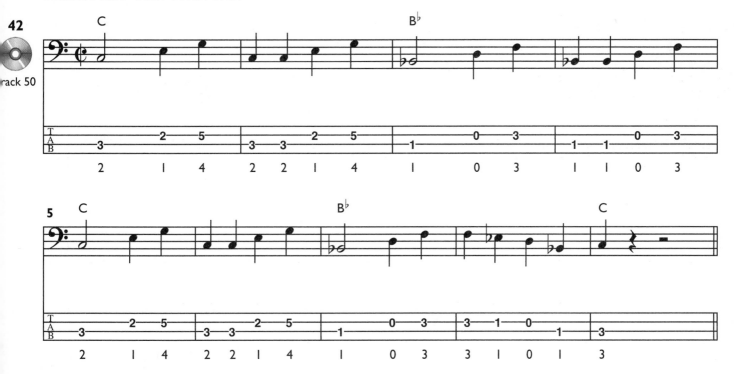

Joey Gittleman of The Mighty Mighty Bosstones

The Mighty Mighty Bosstones formed in 1985 and were largely responsible for popularizing the third wave of ska, which was a combination of ska and hardcore, hence the term *ska-core*. The bassist, Joey Gittleman, started on guitar but switched over to the bass, where he felt more comfortable.

Many ska bands, including The Mighty Mighty Bosstones, have horns as part of the instrumentation of the band. Because of this, songs are often written in the keys of F, B♭, or E♭ because these keys are more "user friendly" for horn players. The first bass line below is in the key of B♭ and is in the style of The Mighty Mighty Bosstones tune "Simmer Down."

The following groove has a walking bass pattern. The harmonic content is still relatively simple, but the feel is slightly different. This line is similar to the one found in The Mighty Mighty Bosstones tune "Zig Zag Dance."

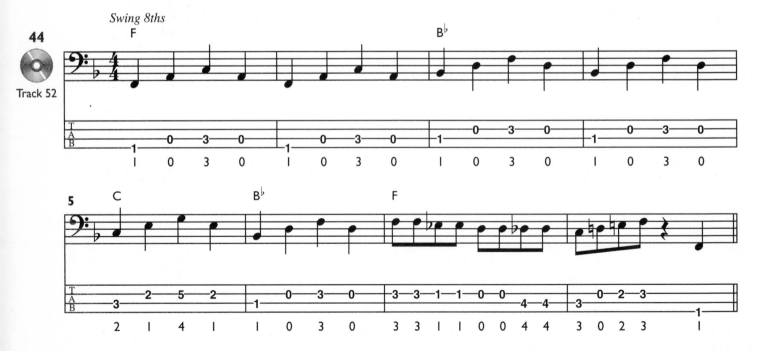

Tony Kanal of No Doubt

No Doubt is a third wave ska band that formed in 1986 in Anaheim, California. They were most successful when integrating reggae and dancehall music into their work. With the releases of the album *Tragic Kingdom* and the single "Just A Girl," No Doubt began to find commercial success. Bassist Tony Kanal did well in playing simply, yet contributing a bass line to the song that was functional and appropriate for the tune. No Doubt had a harder sound than straight ska as they drew from punk, dancehall, and ska influences.

This bass line is in the style of "Just A Girl."

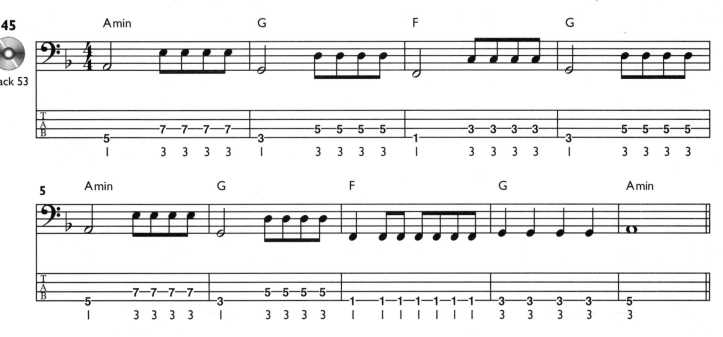

This groove is in the style of "Paulina." In this tune, the guitar plays on the upbeat of every beat of the measure. At fast tempos, it can be challenging for the bassist to play all of the downbeats and the guitarist to play all of the upbeats. On this groove, the bass drum will be playing on all four beats of the measure.

As you have probably found out by now, ska music is a very fun music to play and challenging at the same time with its fast tempos. Try to get together with a couple of friends and play through ska bass lines as the guitarist plays on the upbeats. Have fun!

CHAPTER TEN
OLD SCHOOL FUNK

+ +

Characteristics of Funk Music

Funk music combines elements of soul, jazz, and R&B to create a new genre that's all about the groove. Melody and harmony take a back seat to rhythm. Funk tunes often consist of a single groove that repeats over and over again, usually with only one or two chords. Some funk tunes include a second section called the *bridge* that uses a different rhythm and/or chord progression. Funk grooves can be complex or simple, but they always demand that the bassist keep good time and stay locked in with the drums. The term *old school funk* typically refers to funk from the 1960s and '70s, or to later music that captures the same "vibe."

To understand funk music, you must understand the concept of *syncopation*. When playing less funky styles of music, the bassist typically keeps time by accenting the *onbeats* 1–2–3–4. Syncopation means moving some of the accents to the *offbeats* (the "ands"). Funk bass lines accomplish this by using lots of rests and ties. Be sure to count the sixteenth notes carefully and play the correct rhythms. The best way to understand syncopated funk rhythms is to listen to the classic recordings by the artists discussed in this chapter. And of course, it helps to have a funky drummer to give you that "locked in" feeling.

In the 1960s, James Brown pushed funk music to the forefront with tunes like "Cold Sweat" and "Papa's Got a Brand New Bag." The Meters combined funk with the influence of New Orleans music on tunes like "Cissy Strut." The Isley Brothers bridged the gap of funk and rock with the tune "It's Your Thing." Sly & the Family Stone reached a wide audience with hits like "Dance to the Music."

In the 1970s, George Clinton and his bands Parliament and Funkadelic took funk to a new level. He couldn't have done it without the funky bass playing of Bootsy Collins.

Other prominent old school funk bands (and their bass players) include the Brothers Johnson (Louis Johnson), Tower of Power (Rocco Prestia), Bootsy's Rubber Band (Bootsy Collins), the Ohio Players (Marshall Jones), Earth Wind & Fire (Verdine White), The Commodores (Ronald La Pread), Kool & the Gang (Robert "Kool" Bell), and others. These groups and more are responsible for the emergence of funk bands of today.

Fingerstyle Funk

There are generally two techniques of bass playing used by funk bassists: *fingerstyle funk* and *slap & pop* (which we'll explore on page 64). Fingerstyle funk refers to bass lines that are played using the fingers of the right hand (usually the 1st and 2nd). The fingerstyle technique has a more "traditional" sound and is less percussive than slap & pop. Some of the fingerstyle funk bassists we'll discuss include James Jamerson, Rocco Prestia, and Jaco Pastorius (in the Latin funk section, page 85).

James Jamerson of The Funk Brothers

James Jamerson was a studio bassist who anchored most of the Motown hits of the 1960s and early '70s. He played on an astounding number of hit songs, including "What's Going On" and "I Heard It Through the Grapevine" by Marvin Gaye; "Signed, Sealed, Delivered, I'm Yours," "For Once in My Life," and "I Was Made to Love Her" by Stevie Wonder; "Bernadette" by The Four Tops; and "Ain't No Mountain High Enough" by Marvin Gaye and Tammy Terrell. Check out the movie *Standing in the Shadows of Motown* to learn more about Jamerson and his Motown colleagues The Funk Brothers.

While James Jamerson's work was largely anonymous during his lifetime, his recordings were a huge influence on many bassists and musicians in general. He is widely regarded as a genius for introducing "artistic" bass lines into the realm of pop music. Because of his incredible sense of rhythm, he is considered a founding father of funk. His bass lines were usually syncopated, meaning they danced around the beat rather than keeping strict quarter-note time as most pop bassists had done up until that point.

Muted Notes

Muted notes are an important part of funk bass playing. Remember that funk is more focused on the rhythmic aspect of music than the harmonic or melodic aspects. A muted note is played by plucking the string with the right hand while resting two or more fingers on the string with the left hand. The result is not a particular pitch or note, but more of a percussive sound.

This first groove is similar to the one Jamerson played on "What's Going On."

Listen to the genius of James Jamerson in the following example. This bass line is in the style of the Stevie Wonder classic "For Once in My Life."

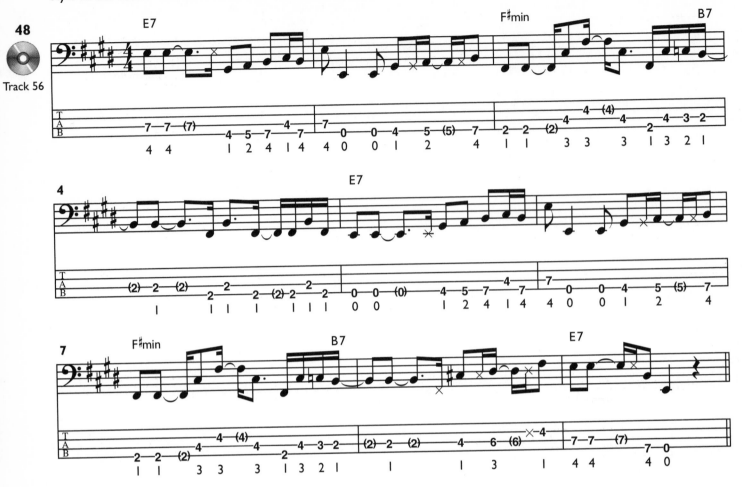

Here's another Jamerson-style groove. Check out the *anticipations* (notes played slightly ahead of the beat), syncopation, and chromatic tones (tones that are not in the scale). This bass line is in the style of the Stevie Wonder tune "I Was Made to Love Her."

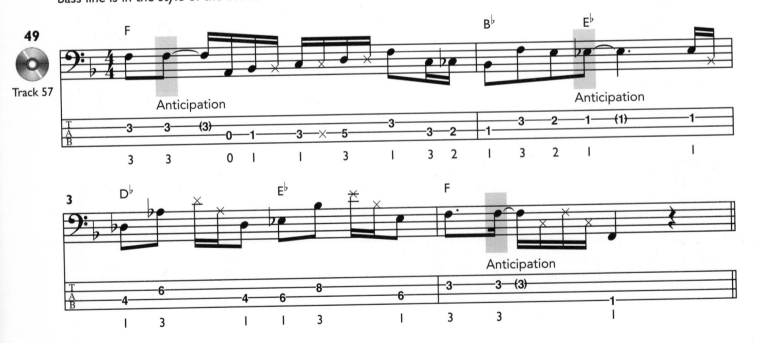

In addition to Jamerson's mastery of syncopation and chromaticism, he also knew how to lay down a simple groove composed of repeated patterns. Check out this example.

50

Track 58

Here is another example of a repeated figure bass line in the style of James Jamerson. This groove is in the style of "Get Ready."

51

Track 59

After you get these bass lines under your fingers, listen to as many Motown recordings as you can to learn from the genius of James Jamerson.

The Bassists of James Brown

Known as "The Godfather of Soul," James Brown was one of the first and most important funksters. Bassists Bernard Odum and Bootsy Collins, among others, had stints in the James Brown band. Odum was in the band from 1958–1969, and Bootsy was with Brown from 1968–1971. In the late 1960s, Brown began to pump out many of the funk and soul anthems still heard on radio stations today. Following are a few funk lines in the style of James Brown.

This one is in the style of James Brown's classic tune "Cold Sweat."

52
Track 60

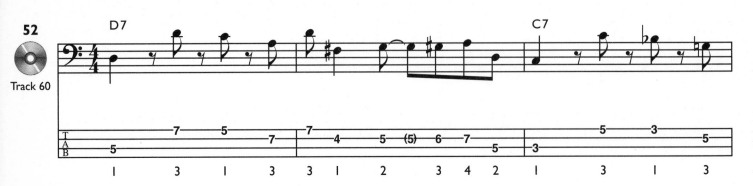

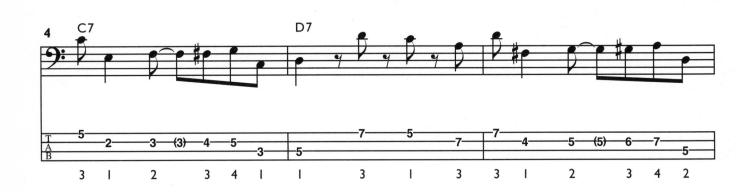

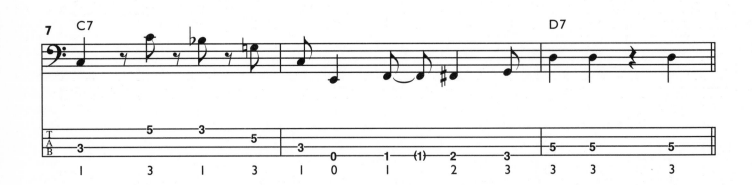

This line is in the style of "Get Up Offa That Thing." The syncopation is tricky, so be sure to count the rhythm carefully, and watch out for the muted notes.

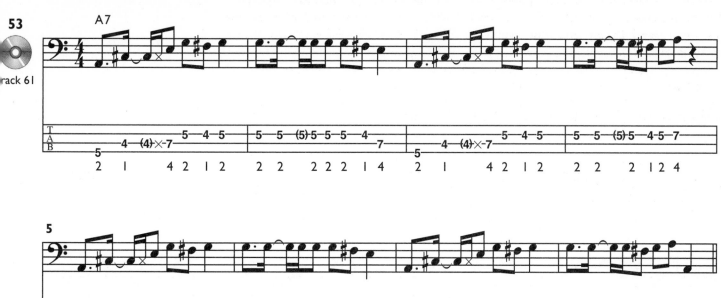

If you listen to a good number of James Brown tunes, you'll find that many of the bass lines are similar in note choice and rhythms, and many of the tunes are in the same key, but they are all *funky*. Here is another example in the style of James Brown.

George Porter Jr. of The Meters

The Meters formed in the New Orleans area in 1965. In 1969, they released one of their better known tunes, "Cissy Strut." Though the band did not achieve the level of commercial success that James Brown and others enjoyed, The Meters are considered one of the originators of funk.

George Porter Jr. began playing bass with The Meters when the group formed in 1965. In addition to holding down the bottom for the group, Porter also worked with the likes of Paul McCartney, Dr. John, Jimmy Buffet, Patti Labelle, David Byrne, and others. Check out George's funky riffs on tunes such as "Cissy Strut" or "Funky Miracle."

Here is a bass line in the style of George Porter Jr. and The Meters.

Here's another example in the style of George Porter Jr. and The Meters.

Many of the riffs played in Meters tunes are derived from the minor pentatonic scale. Here is another bass line using a minor pentatonic riff.

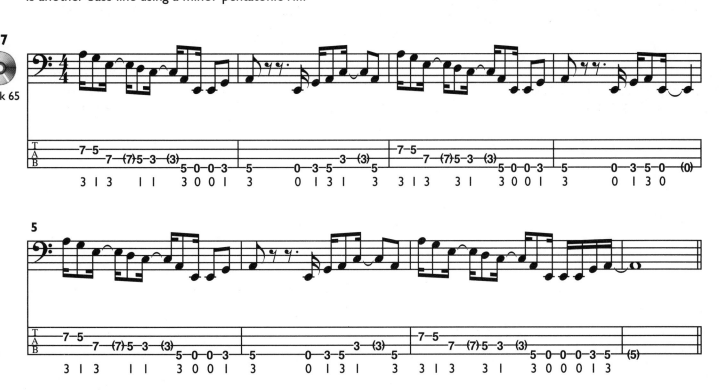

Verdine White of Earth, Wind & Fire

Verdine White is the bassist for Earth, Wind & Fire, a popular funk band of the 1970s. Verdine's energetic grooves drove such tunes as "Shining Star" and "September."

Here is a groove in the style of Verdine White. Notice the use of *grace notes* ♪. A grace note embellishes the note it precedes and helps add flavor to the line.

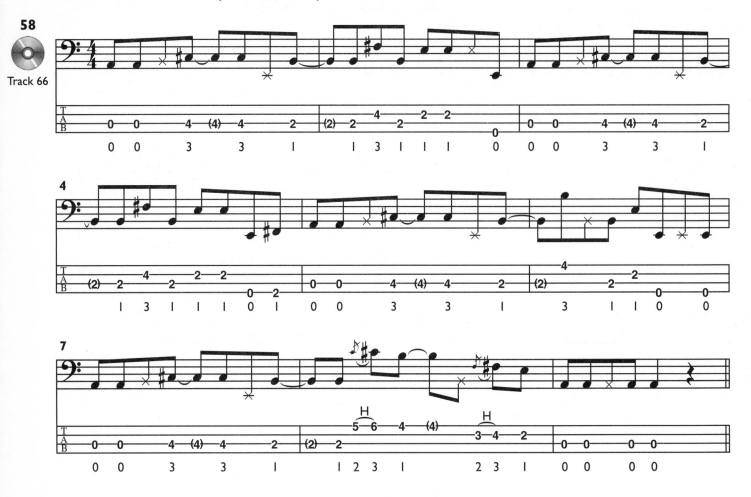

Here is another bass line in the style of Verdine White. Note the *double stops* that appear in bars 2 and 6. A double stop is two notes played at the same time.

62   The Bass Style Resource

Rocco Prestia of Tower of Power

Rocco Prestia is one of the masters of fingerstyle funk and is known for his work with the legendary funk group Tower of Power. His left-hand technique is unique in that Rocco uses his 1st and 2nd fingers to fret the notes and his 3rd and 4th fingers to slightly mute the notes and cut down on sustain. The result is halfway between a muted note and a regular note. This technique, along with his signature sixteenth notes played with the right hand, produce very percussive sounding bass lines. Check out some of the great Rocco bass lines found on tunes such as "What Is Hip?," "Squib Cakes," and "Only So Much Oil in the Ground."

The bass lines below are in the style of Rocco Prestia. His bass lines feature incredible grooves that are more about the sixteenth-note pulse and rhythm than the notes themselves.

This one is in the style of the tune "Only So Much Oil in the Ground."

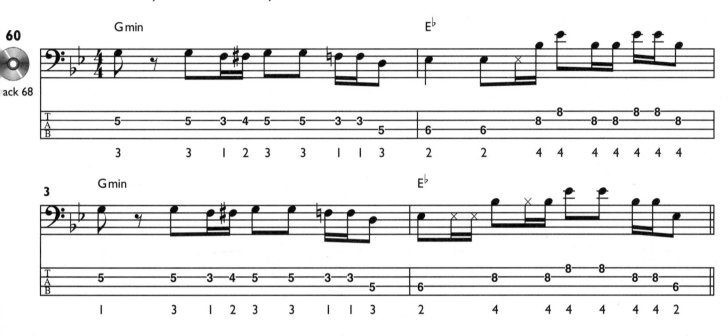

The following is another sixteenth-note groove in the style of Rocco Prestia. Note the octaves that occur in bars 2 and 4. This line is similar to one that Rocco plays in the tune "What Is Hip?"

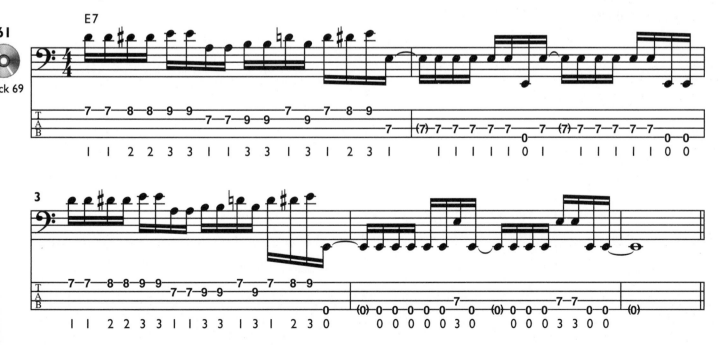

The Slap & Pop Style

The *slap & pop* technique has become very popular since Larry Graham (see page 65) introduced it to the world of funk. This percussive effect is produced using two main techniques: slapping the string with the right-hand thumb and popping the string with the right-hand 1st finger. The style also makes use of muted notes, hammer-ons, and pull-offs.

Other funk bassists who helped popularize the slap & pop technique include Louis Johnson and Bootsy Collins. Stanley Clarke introduced the slap technique to jazz-influenced music in the 1970s. In recent years, Flea (The Red Hot Chili Peppers), Mark King (Level 42), Marcus Miller (Miles Davis), Stu Hamm (Joe Satriani), Les Claypool (Primus), Victor Wooten (Béla Fleck), and others have taken the technique to new heights.

SLAP & POP TECHNIQUES	
S	**Thumb slap:** Strike the string with your right-hand thumb. The string should make a percussive sound as it strikes the fretboard.
P	**Pop:** Pluck or "pop" the string with the 1st (or 2nd, as we'll discuss on page 74) finger of your right hand. The string will snap back and strike the fretboard, creating a sharp, percussive sound.
H	**Hammer-on:** Play a lower-pitched note normally, then play a higher-pitched note on the same string by "hammering" onto the fret with your left-hand finger. Do not use your right hand; the sound comes from the left hand alone.
PO	**Pull-off:** A pull-off is the opposite of a hammer-on. Play a higher-pitched note normally, then play a lower-pitched note on the same string by quickly pulling your left-hand finger off the fret. Do not use your right hand; the sound comes from the left hand alone.
SL or SL	**Slide:** Play the first note normally, then slide up or down to a second note by moving your left hand while maintaining pressure on the fretboard. Do not use your right hand; the sound comes from the left hand alone.
x	**Muted note:** While using the indicated right-hand technique, rest your left-hand fingers lightly on the strings (without pressing them to the fretboard). The desired effect is a "thump" sound that does not have an actual pitch.

For a more in-depth look at the slap & pop style, refer to the book *Slap & Pop Bass* (by Dave Overthrow, #21904).

To make the examples easier to read, the bass lines in this chapter assume you are using the thumb (S) technique unless otherwise noted.

Now, let's look at some examples. Nothing gets people dancing like a funky slap & pop bass line.

Larry Graham

Larry Graham is best known for his work with Sly & the Family Stone, and he also led his own group called Graham Central Station. More recently, he has worked with Prince. Graham's signature bass lines anchor songs such as "Thank You (Falettinme Be Mice Elf Agin)," "I Want to Take You Higher," "Simple Song," and "Stand."

In the following slap bass lines, you will notice the slap & pop notation above each note. Remember, any note without a symbol is to be played by the thumb.

This groove is in the style of the Sly and the Family Stone tune "Thank You."

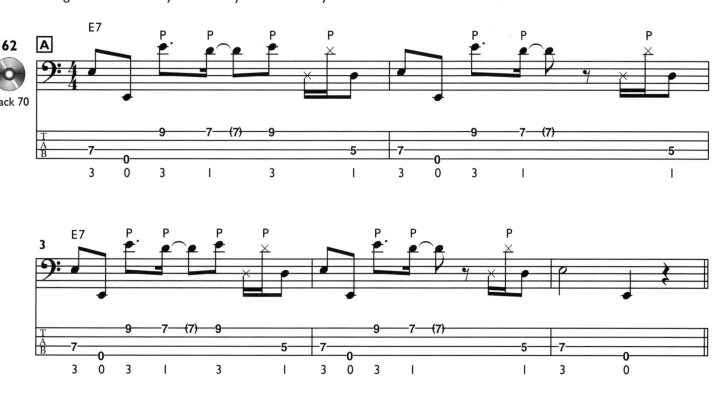

Here's another great example of slap & pop bass in the style of Larry Graham.

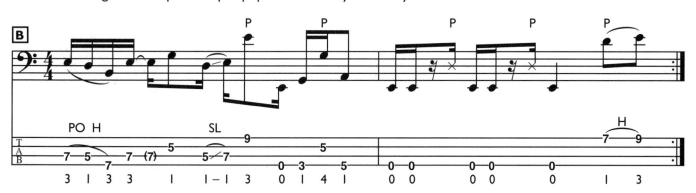

This example is in the style of the Graham Central Station song "The Jam." The hammer-ons add some funk to this great-sounding line; play through it slowly at first.

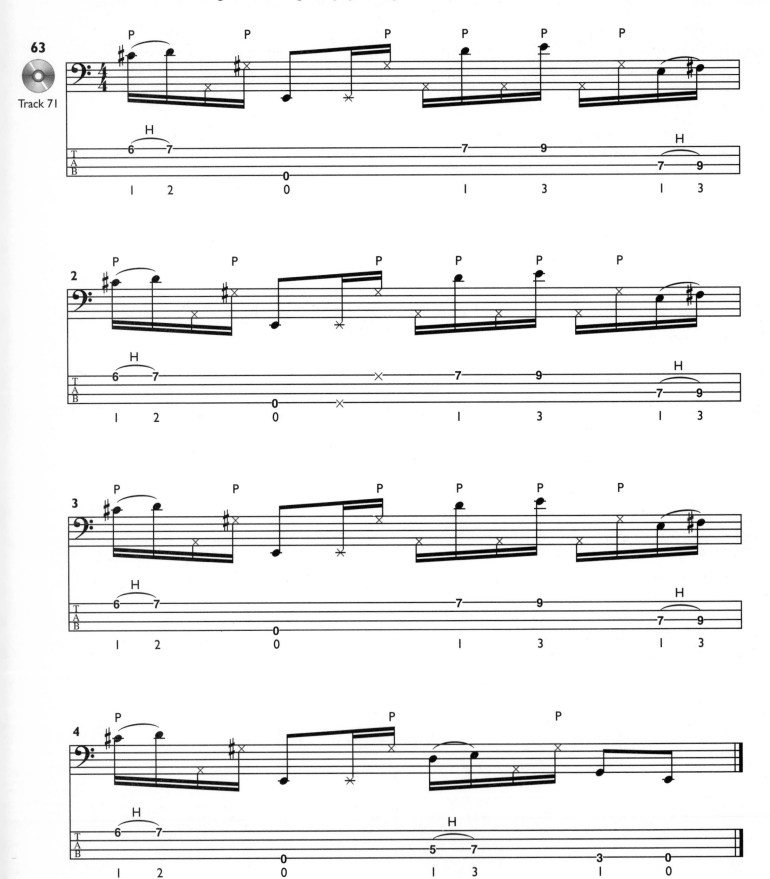

The following groove is in the style of the Larry Graham tune "Feel the Need." Concentrate on really getting the slides down on this one.

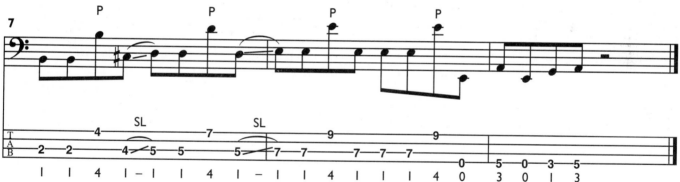

Various Old-School Grooves

Following are slap & pop lines in the styles of various artists and groups. The first one is in the style of "Brick House" by The Commodores.

The next example is in the style of "Shakey Ground" by The Temptations.

Here is one more old-school funk slap & pop line.

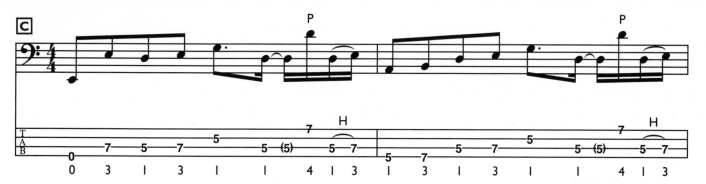

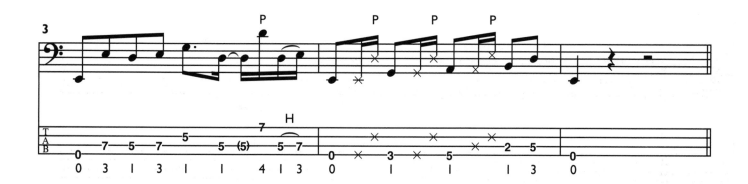

After you have the bass lines in this chapter under your fingers, try to create some funk bass lines of your own.

CHAPTER ELEVEN
MODERN FUNK SLAP & POP

+ +

Since Larry Graham popularized the slap & pop style in the 1960s and '70s, the technique has continued to evolve. Over the last three or four decades, we have seen many great bassists take the slap technique further and come up with their own styles and techniques. Mark King, Marcus Miller, Flea, Stanley Clarke, and Victor Wooten all have flawless technique and have developed slap & pop styles of their own. Stanley Clarke was one of the first to slap over complex chord changes. Flea of The Red Hot Chili Peppers brought slap into the mainstream rock arena. Mark King displayed his amazing slap & pop bass in the pop-rock band Level 42. Marcus Miller slaps and pops with amazing musicality. Victor Wooten dazzles us with his *double thumping* and *double plucking* (see page 74). The double thumping and double plucking techniques are the main characteristics of modern funk slap & pop. On the following pages, we'll examine bass lines in the styles of some of the bassists mentioned above. When playing the bass lines, take them slow and have fun.

Modern Funk Slap & Pop Lines

Marcus Miller

Marcus Miller is probably best known for his work with Miles Davis, David Sanborn, Luther Vandross, and his own band, but he has appeared on countless recordings with many other artists. Marcus is one of the premier bassists in the industry and a master of the slap & pop style. He often uses sixteenth-note triplets in his lines. Marcus also uses the left hand to mute notes in many patterns that he plays. In the bass on the next page, the sixteenth-note triplets require a thumb (slap), then a *muted hammer-on*, and then a pluck. A muted hammer-on is produced by striking or "slapping" the strings using two or more fingers of the left hand. Strike the strings hard enough to produce a muted, percussive sound, but not so hard that they strike the fretboard. This technique is often used to create muted notes when playing rhythms of short duration at fast tempos.

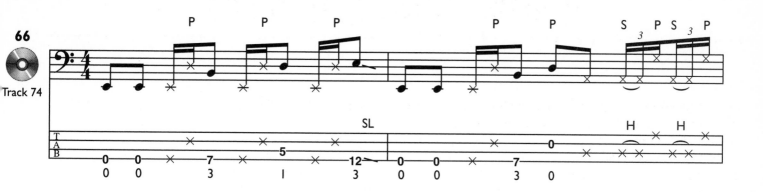

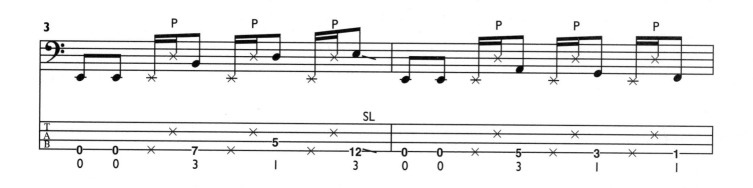

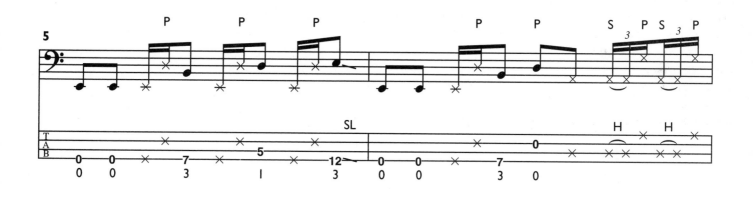

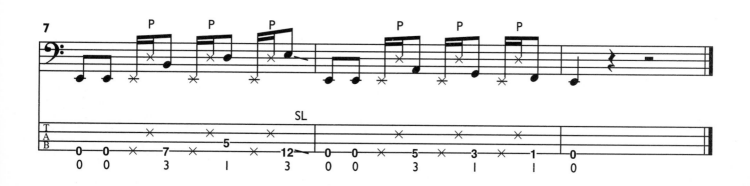

Flea of The Red Hot Chili Peppers

Flea, the bassist for The Red Hot Chili Peppers, took funk and the slap & pop style and crossed over into the rock genre. His bass lines are a distinctive part of the group's sound.

Following is a funk bass line in the style of Flea. Note the use of triplets in this line, reminiscent of the Stevie Wonder tune "Higher Ground."

Here is another bass line in the style of Flea. This groove is in the style of the Chili Peppers tune "Aeroplane."

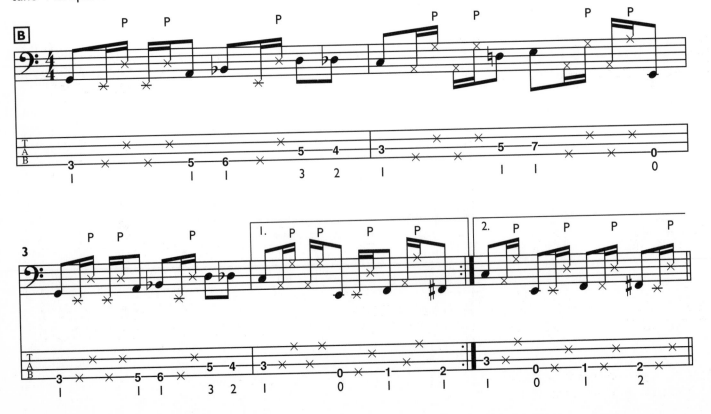

Mark King of Level 42

The British pop band Level 42 had a number of hits in the 1980s. They are well-known for their musical abilities, in particular their bassist Mark King. Level 42 took powerful funk and fusion-influenced grooves and incorporated them into pop music. Some Level 42 hits include "Chinese Way," "When the Sun Goes Down," and "Something About You." In addition to recording many albums as bassist and lead vocalist of Level 42, Mark has also recorded several solo recordings. Following are slap & pop funk bass lines in the style of Mark King.

In the following example, the thumb symbol (S) has been included in bar 4 for clarity when playing the sixteenth-note triplets.

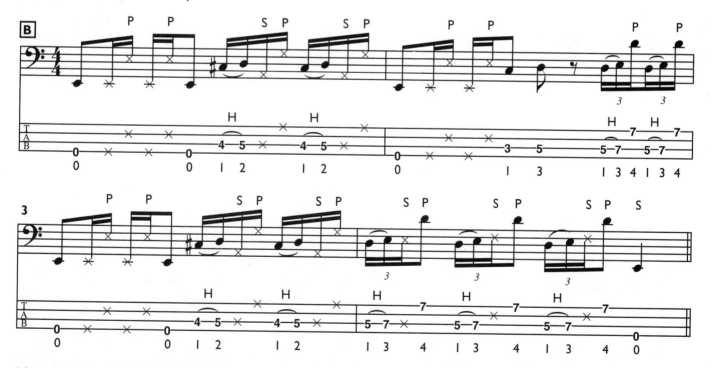

After you get these bass lines under your fingers, try to invent some of your own incorporating sixteenth-note triplets.

Victor Wooten

Victor Wooten is best known for his work with Béla Fleck and the Flecktones and his solo recordings, but he has also worked with many others in a variety of genres. Wooten often uses double thumping and double popping, and has inspired many young bassists to pursue these techniques.

Double plucking—Pluck (pop) with both the 1st and 2nd fingers of the right hand. The symbols below are used for double plucking situations.

> P1 = Pluck with the 1st finger of the right hand
> P2 = Pluck with the 2nd finger of the right hand

Double thumping—This is when you pluck both downwards and upwards with your thumb to produce notes.

> T1 = Thumb Downstroke (slap)
> T2 = Thumb Upstroke

Below are bass lines in the style of Victor Wooten. Play them slowly at first to ensure you play each note correctly in both pitch and rhythm. Note the use of double plucking. Since all of the thumb (slap) notes are downstrokes, the (S) symbol is excluded for ease of reading.

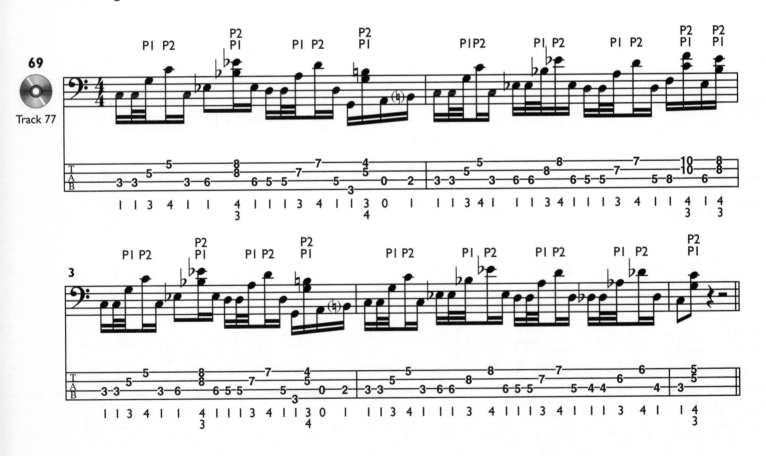

This bass line is in the style of Victor Wooten and demonstrates the double thumping technique that he uses.

Various Lines Using Double Thumping and Double Plucking

This one uses the double thumping technique.

The double plucking technique is used in the example that follows.

This bass line uses both double thumping and double plucking.

CHAPTER TWELVE
JAZZ—WALKING BASS

+++

A *walking bass* line usually consists of quarter notes and usually moves by steps. Unlike walking bass parts in blues, which often consist of repeated patterns, walking bass lines in jazz are improvisational by nature and rarely consist of repeated figures. Jazz also uses more involved harmonic structures than the blues and allows the bassist to use chord tones, chord scales, passing tones, and approach notes more freely (all of these concepts will be explained throughout this chapter). Creating jazz walking bass lines is, in effect, soloing with quarter notes.

In order to create an effective jazz walking bass line, the bassist should be familiar with chord structures, chord scales, and the modes. Walking bass lines can be constructed with chord tones only, and this would be technically correct, however, intermediate and advanced walking bass lines use scale tones and other techniques and concepts such as *passing tones* and *approach notes* in order to provide for the smooth *stepwise motion* that is associated with a jazz walking bass line. Stepwise motion means using half steps and whole steps rather than larger intervals. One way to accomplish this is to use a passing tone, which is a non-chord tone that connects two notes by stepwise motion. Another is to use an approach note, which is a non-chord tone a half step or whole step above or below the note that follows. Jazz players typically use passing tones and approach notes on beats 2 and 4 to set up chord tones on beats 3 and 1.

Following is an example of a walking bass line in the blues genre and then a walking bass line in the jazz genre. Notice how much more stepwise motion there is in the jazz walking bass line.

Walking Bass Line in a Blues Style

In the jazz bass line that follows, the passing tones are highlighted and indicated by the letter P, and the approach tones by the letter A.

Walking Bass Line in a Jazz Style

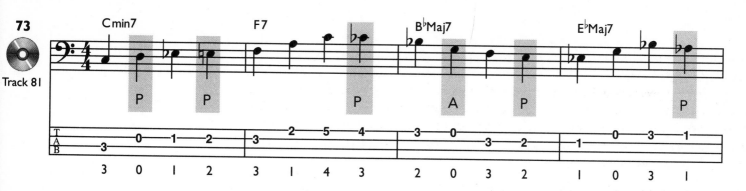

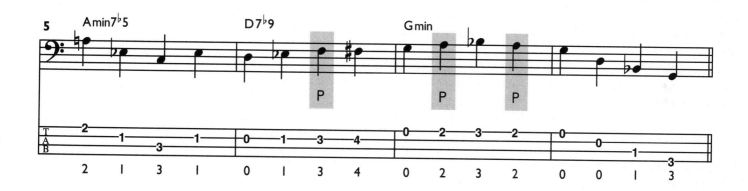

Notice the different textures of each bass line. The blues bass line consists strictly of chord tones, whereas the jazz walking line uses chromatic tones and stepwise motion.

Beginning Walking Bass Lines—Chord Tones

Walking bass lines that consist of chord tones are functional and will nicely outline the quality of each chord. Try to become familiar with all of the triads and 7th chord types so you know what notes to play on each chord (see page 11). When playing over progressions with two chords per bar, using chord tones is a logical choice because we can only play two tones per chord. This usually results in one of the following choices: root and 5th; root and 3rd; or root and 7th.

Here is an example of a tune using two chords per bar with each receiving two beats.

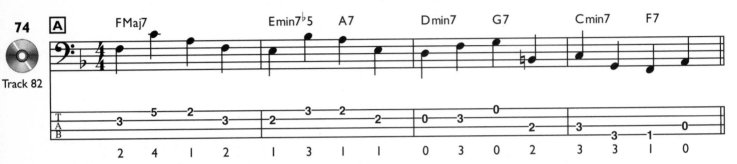

When you have one chord per bar, you can play four quarter notes to outline the chord sound. Here is an example of a tune using one chord per bar.

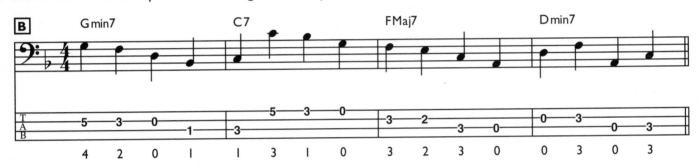

Here is a walking bass line over a standard chord progression using chord tones. When playing this line, notice how the chord is outlined by playing each note of the chord. Soloists in a jazz band love to hear the simplicity of a bass line using chord tones because the harmony is clearly stated in the bass line, and this makes it comfortable to solo over.

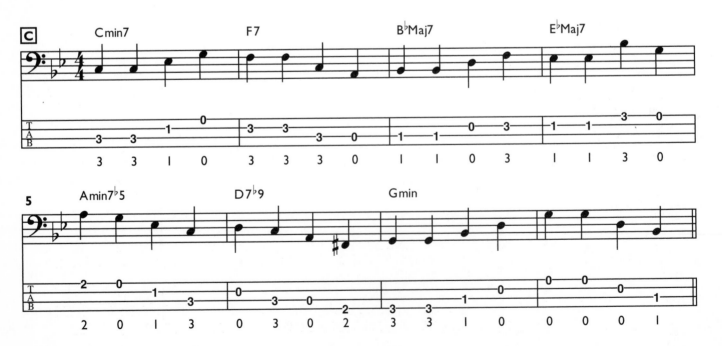

Intermediate Walking Bass Lines—Scale Tones

To take the next step in creating a walking bass line, we will incorporate scale tones. Using scale tones provides for smoother motion and allows us to connect the chord tones.

The bass lines below are based over diatonic chord progressions, meaning all of the chords are within the key. The blues progressions we looked at previously are not diatonic progressions, because they used three different dominant 7th chords. In diatonic harmony, there is only one dominant chord per key.

Here is an example using scale tones to connect chord tones. In this example, the connecting scale tones are highlighted.

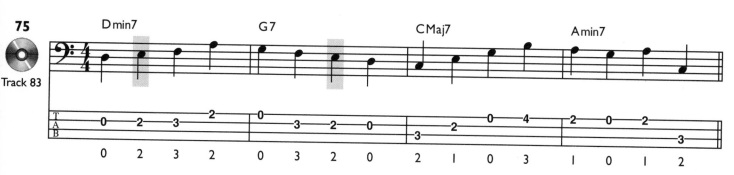

There are often several scale choices for a chord, especially dominant 7th chords. Review the scale chart (page 21). The following are scale choices commonly used when creating walking bass lines.

1. Major chords—Major scale
2. Minor chords—Dorian mode
3. Dominant chords—Mixolydian mode
4. Minor 7♭5 chords—Locrian mode

The list above includes some of the more common choices, but when you study the chord chart, you will discover more options. The more familiar you are with these scales, the more effective you will be in creating great sounding walking bass lines.

Following is a walking bass line using scale tones. Notice how the bass line sounds smoother than when we used chord tones exclusively.

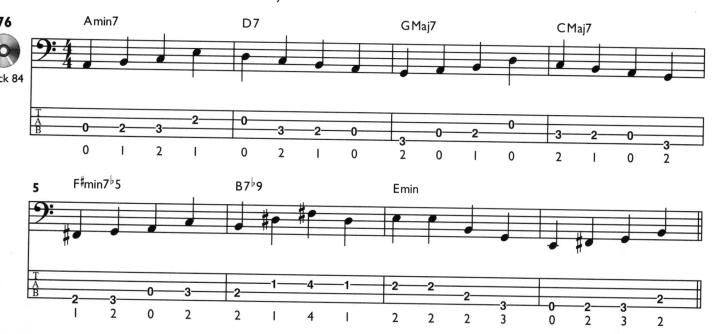

Advanced Walking Bass Lines—Approach Notes, Chromatic Tones, and Rhythmic Activity

So far, we have discussed walking bass lines that are diatonic. Approach notes and chromatic tones give us notes that are non-diatonic and help provide tension and release in the bass line. The chromatic tones and half-step approach tones also allow for a smooth half-step motion.

Below is an example with half-step approach notes (highlighted). Each new chord is approached by a tone one half step above.

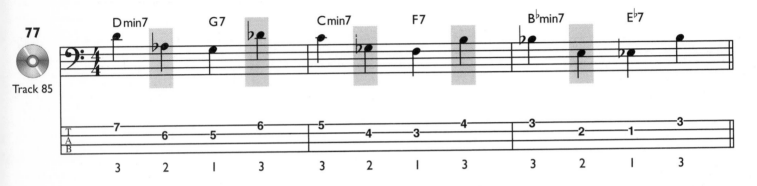

Chromatic tones are commonly used in walking bass lines to connect two scale tones and provide a "darker" sound in your bass lines. Here is an example using chromatic tones (highlighted).

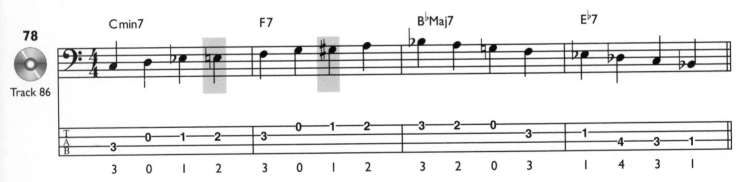

Now, let's play a walking bass line using both approach notes and chromatic tones over a blues in F.

Blue Neighbors
Track 87

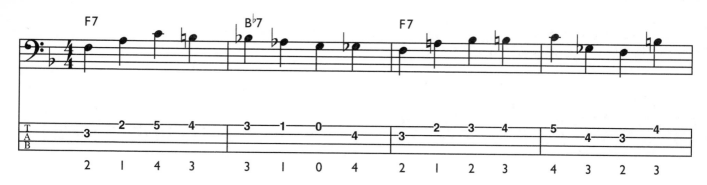

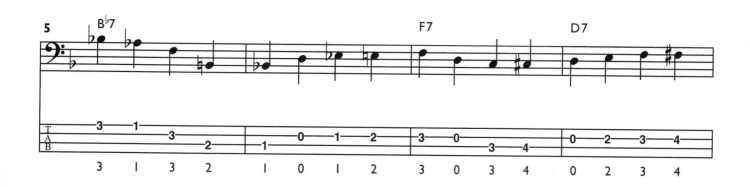

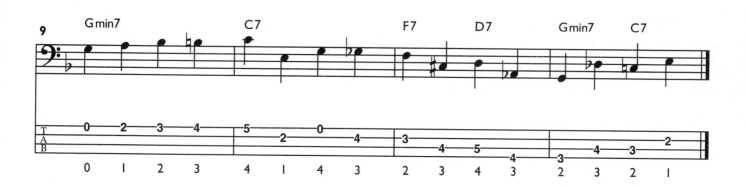

CHAPTER THIRTEEN
LATIN BASS LINES

++

Bossa Nova

Bossa nova originated in Brazil and, in the 1950s, was introduced into American jazz. The bossa nova bass part typically uses the root and 5th of the chord and a dotted quarter-note/eighth-note rhythm, as in the following example.

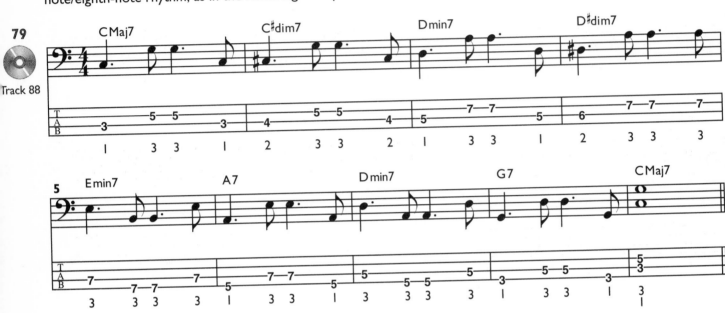

Samba

Samba is Brazil's most popular style of music and dance. The difference between the bossa nova and the samba is, although they share similar rhythms, the samba style is played with a double-time feel. The piece below is written in cut time (see page 50), which means you should count the beat as 1, 2; 1, 2 rather than 1, 2, 3, 4; 1, 2, 3, 4.

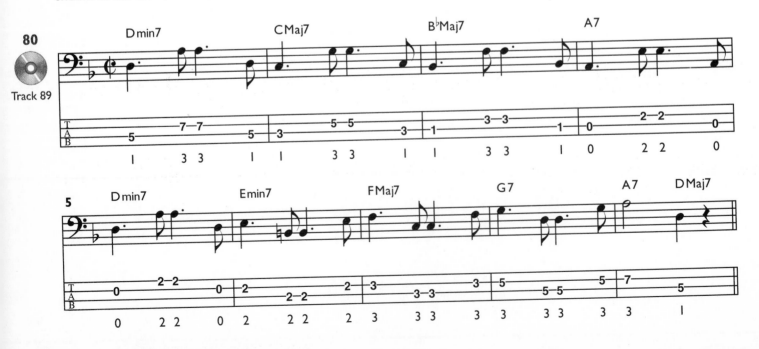

Latin Funk in the Style of Jaco Pastorius

Latin, Afro-Cuban, and Caribbean styles such as the bossa nova, samba, cha-cha-chá, calypso, and others have found their way into American mainstream funk. Jaco Pastorius, known for his extraordinary bass playing with Weather Report, Pat Metheny, and his own big band, was one of the most influential electric bassists. Jaco played incredibly funky bass lines, and often his sixteenth-note funk grooves were influenced by Latin and island music. The following examples are all in the style of Jaco Pastorius.

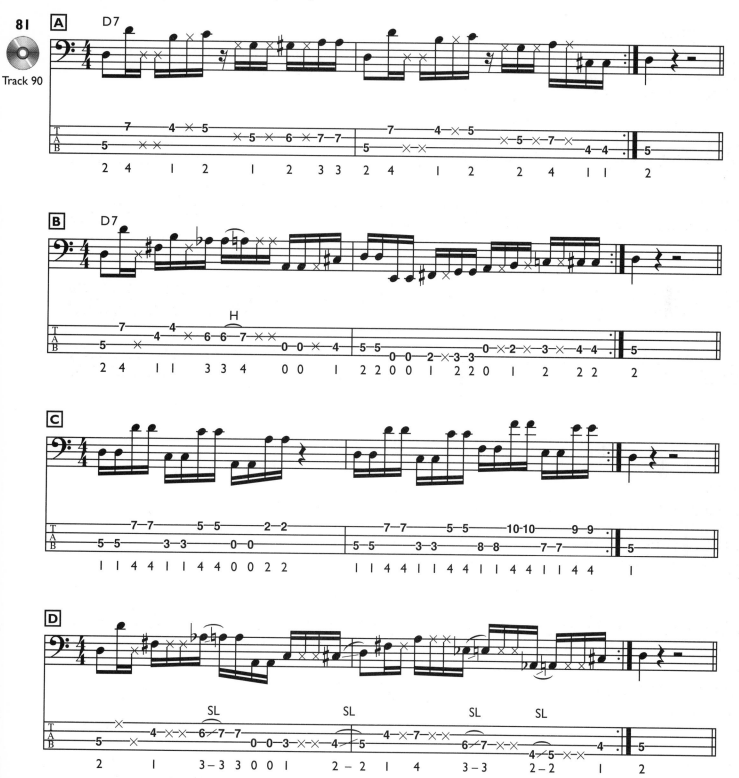

CHAPTER FOURTEEN
PLAYING CHORDS ON THE BASS

++

As the role of modern electric bass has expanded over the years, bass players in certain situations sometimes find themselves playing chords on the bass. Listen to Stanley Clarke on "School Days" or Jaco on his version of the Paul McCartney tune "Blackbird." Listen to Roscoe Beck play chords behind a Robben Ford blues guitar solo.

If you are interested in continuing your chord studies, check out *The Bass Chord Encyclopedia* (by Tracy Walton, #24409). You might also consider an *extended range bass* such as a five- or six-string for even more possibilities. In this chapter, however, we will focus on some basic triads and 7th chords on the four-string bass.

Triads

Although there are four types of triads, those most often played as chords on the bass are major triads and minor triads. Below are fingerings for each type of chord. In the third voicing shown for each type of triad, the 5th is replaced by the octave.

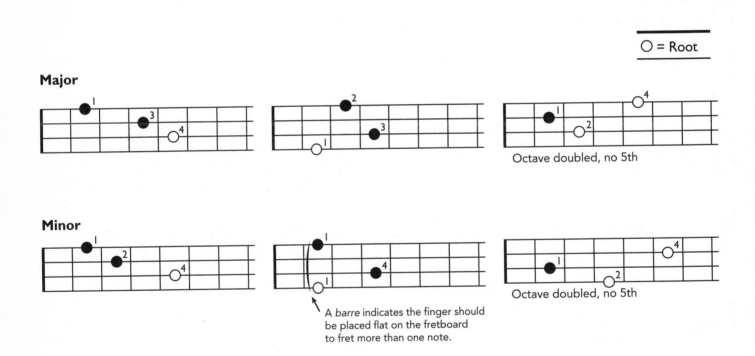

7th Chords

The most useful 7th chords on the bass are major 7th, dominant 7th, and minor 7th. Below are fingerings for each of these types. The 5th is typically omitted when playing 7th chords on the bass. The root, 3rd, and 7th are the important notes that define the chord.

Major 7th

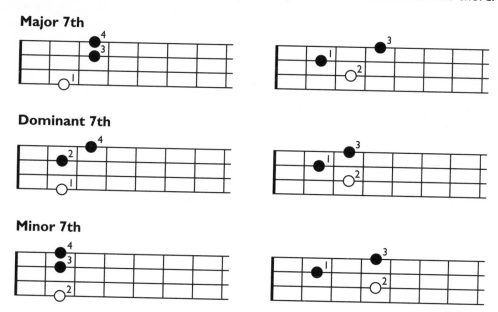

Dominant 7th

Minor 7th

Chordal Pieces

Let's take a look at a couple of Latin funk grooves that incorporate chords.

Here is a two-chord funk vamp using a minor 7th chord and a dominant 7th chord. The part is simple, but effective.

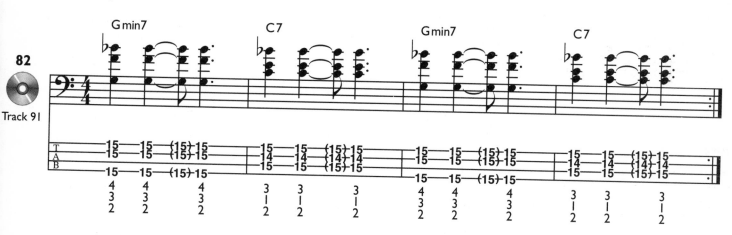

Here is a I–vi–ii–V progression using major 7th, minor 7th, and dominant 7th chords.

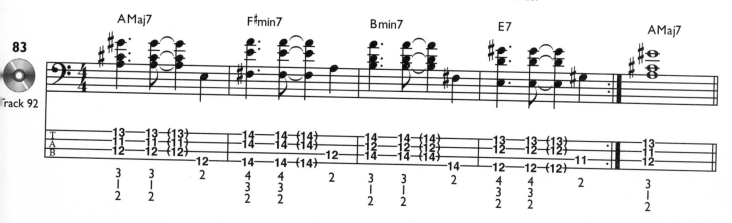

Finally, here is a 12-bar blues using voicings of dominant 7th chords. This blues progression is a jazz blues that includes the ii–V–I turnaround. Also, notice that the dotted quarter notes are played *staccato* (in a short, detached way). Play this through slowly at first to make sure you get all the correct notes.

Funk Rock Groove

Track 93

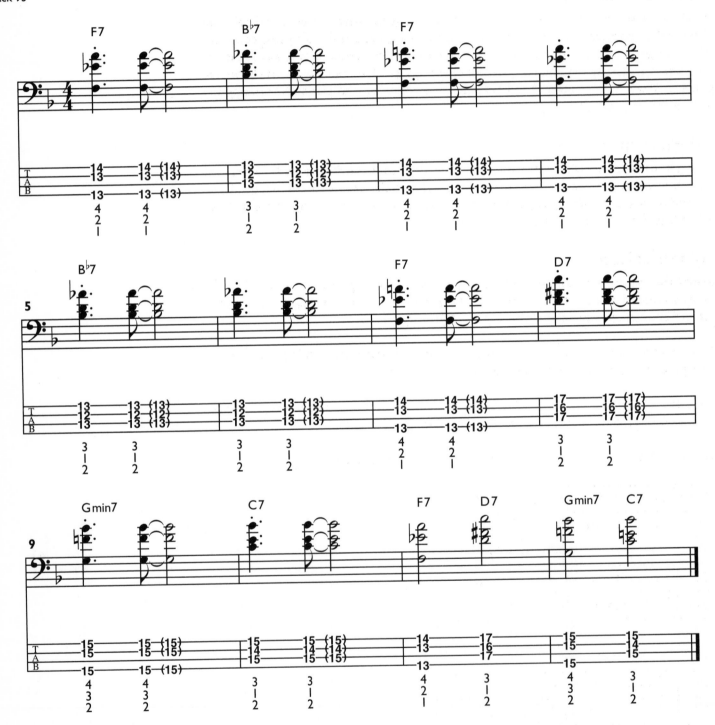

Once these chordal pieces are under your fingers, try coming up with a few of your own. Also, try taking tunes you know and working out the chord progression using chords instead of bass lines. Try mixing it up—use chords for a few bars, break into a bass line, then go back into chords. Experiment.

CHAPTER FIFTEEN
TAPPING CHORDS ON THE BASS

+ +

Two-Hand Tapping

Two-hand tapping is a technique that has been used by guitar players ever since Eddie Van Halen helped popularize the technique. As the name implies, two-hand tapping combines left- and right-hand tapping. In recent years, tapping has been adopted by bassists (such as the great rock bassist Billy Sheehan) for not only playing melody, but also to play harmony. Listen to Victor Wooten or Michael Manring use the technique to play both harmony and melody simultaneously!

Left-Hand Tapping

To tap a note with the left hand, use your 1st finger to attack the A note on the 5th fret of the 4th string. Use a swift motion to press the string to the fretboard with enough force to produce a sound. After you get a pitch, practice tapping various notes of the 3rd and 4th strings with your 1st, 2nd, and 3rd fingers.

Right-Hand Tapping

Right-hand tapping is similar to left-hand tapping, except the right hand has to be in front of the fretboard to execute the technique. Attempt to tap several different notes on the 1st and 2nd strings with each of the fingers of your right hand.

After you are comfortable getting notes out of this technique with each hand, turn to the next page and attempt to play "Aqua Bossa."

This bass part includes a bass line in the left hand and chords in the right hand. The part is based on a standard bossa nova tune. Take it slow and have fun.

Below is a legend of two-hand tapping notation you will encounter.

Notation Legend for Two-Hand Tapping	
R1	Tap with right-hand index finger
R2	Tap with right-hand middle finger
R3	Tap with right-hand ring finger
R4	Tap with right-hand little finger
R5	Tap with right-hand thumb
L1	Tap with left-hand index finger
L2	Tap with left-hand middle finger
L3	Tap with left-hand ring finger
L4	Tap with right-hand little finger

Aqua Bossa

Track 94

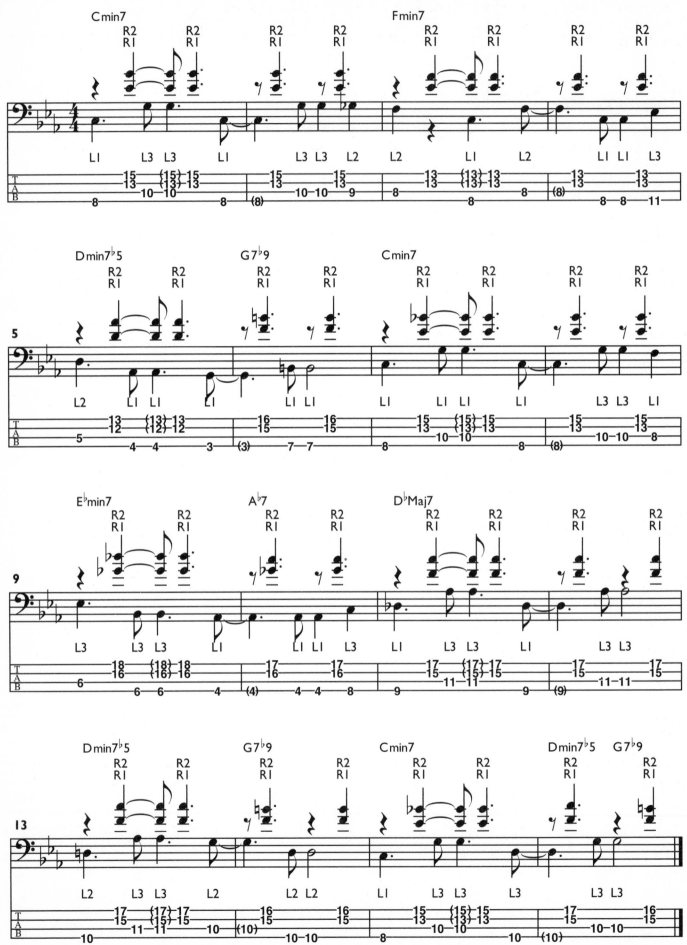

Tapping a Shuffle Blues

Here is another piece that utilizes the two-handed tapping technique. Although you may have played these two parts separately by playing the bass line or the chords, it's now time to combine them. Use your left hand to play the bass line and your right hand to tap out the chords.

Tapping the Blues

Track 95

CHAPTER SIXTEEN
LICKS AND SOLOING

+ +

Traditionally, the role of the bassist is to groove with the drummer. As the role of the instrument has evolved over time, however, it is sometimes appropriate, or even expected, for the bassist to step forward and take a turn in the spotlight. This chapter will teach you some licks and soloing concepts to help you become a more versatile bassist.

Rock Licks with the Minor Pentatonic Scale

The first scales that rock and blues players learn are the minor pentatonic scale and the blues scale. To review these important scales, refer to page 19. Following are some minor pentatonic licks that you might find in a rock bass solo.

D Minor Pentatonic Lick

84
Track 96

G Minor Pentatonic Lick

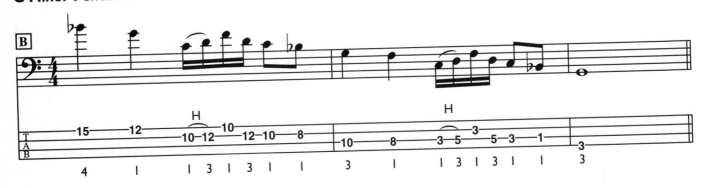

E Minor Pentatonic Lick

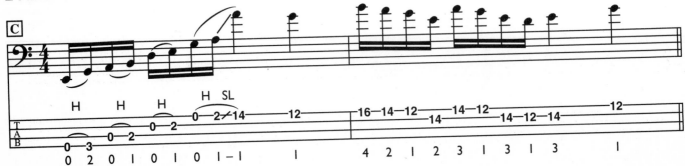

Blues Scale Licks

The blues scale, as the name indicates, is the primary scale used in blues music. The blues scale is similar to the minor pentatonic scale, as it contains the same scale degrees with the addition of the ♭5. The blues scale is also used frequently in rock and jazz music. Below are blues scale licks you can use and incorporate into your solos.

A Blues Scale Lick

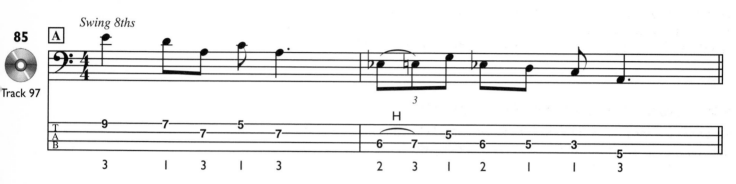

E Blues Scale Lick

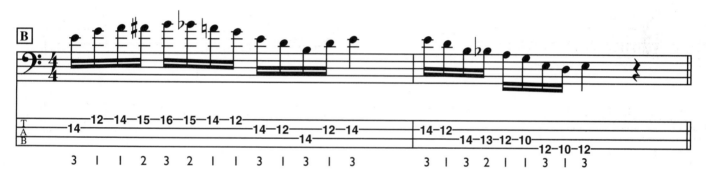

G Blues Scale Lick

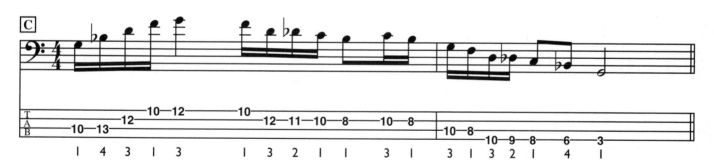

B♭ Blues Scale Lick

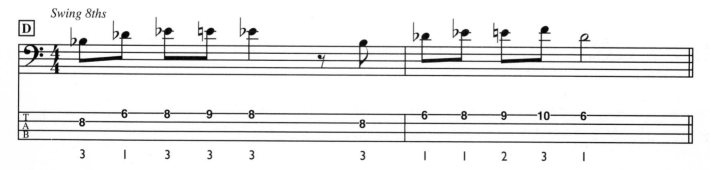

Dorian Scale Licks

The Dorian mode consists of the same scale degrees as the minor pentatonic scale with the addition of a major 2nd and a major 6th (page 16). These two additional tones provide for more color and variety in your solo licks. The Dorian mode is commonly used by jazz musicians as well as rock and blues players. Below are some Dorian mode licks you can use in your solos.

D Dorian Lick

86
Track 98

E Dorian Lick

A Dorian Lick

C Dorian Lick

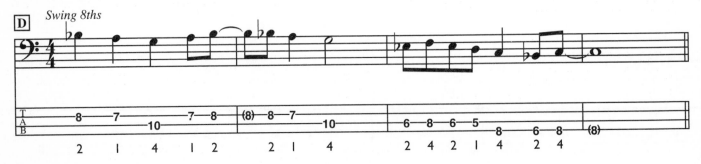

When you get the preceding minor pentatonic, blues scale, and Dorian licks under your fingers, try to work them into your solos. Then, see if you can create some licks of your own using these scales.

Bass Solo

The bass solo below incorporates licks from the minor pentatonic scale, blues scale, and Dorian mode. Although this solo is in the rock style, these scales can be used to create solos in other styles such as jazz, blues, or funk. You can use the same notes and scales, just change the groove and feel to fit the new style.

After you get this solo under your fingers, try to create licks of your own using the three scales mentioned above.

Conclusion

This concludes *The Bass Styles Resource*. By now, you should have a wide range of techniques, grooves, and styles under your belt. You will be well-prepared to face new musical situations with confidence and an open mind. Good luck!